Easy Bicycle Maintenance

by the editors of *Bicycling*® Magazine

Rodale Press, Emmaus, Pennsylvania

Senior Editor, Ray Wolf
Edited by Larry McClung
Cover photograph by Chris Barone
Cover design by Linda Jacopetti and Karen A. Schell
Book design by Linda Jacopetti

Library of Congress Cataloging in Publication Data
Main entry under title:

Easy bicycle maintenance.

　　Cover title: Bicycling magazine's easy bicycle maintenance.
　　1. Bicycles—Maintenance and repair.　I. Bicycling!
II. Title: Bicycling magazine's easy bicycle maintenance.
TL430.E26　　1985　　629.28′772　　85-2184
ISBN 0-87857-544-8　paperback

　　6　8　10　9　7　　　　　　paperback

Contents

Introduction

There's nothing sadder than a bike with mechanical damage. The would-be cyclist finds that he or she will need to spend a considerable sum of money and wait a couple of weeks before taking another ride.

But experienced cyclists seldom have this trouble. They ride their favorite bike year in and year out, knowing they can depend on their bike to be ready whenever they are. Do they know something beginners don't? You bet. They know the importance of preventive maintenance.

You'll find your new bike has other personality traits for you to get used to. Cables will stretch and need to be retightened; spokes will settle in and stretch. As the spokes get looser, the wheel will fall out of true and become weaker. The headset bearings will loosen, giving you a terrible, jittery feeling in the steering and front wheel braking until you retighten the headset locknut. Other nuts and bolts, too numerous to mention, will loosen up. Your chain will need regular lubrication and cleaning.

Dealing with these little quirks is quite easy to learn, and once you know how, it's quite fast. Knowing how to do your own minor repairs and regular maintenance will make cycling far more practical and enjoyable. Many bike shops offer a free 30-day check. Don't turn it down. If possible, arrange to bring your bike in during nonpeak hours and ask to watch the mechanic make the check. You're bound to learn something.

Not all new-bike troubles are mechanical in origin. One common source of trouble for new cyclists is their limited riding experience. When you buy a new bike, you're amazed and delighted at how fast it will go. You want to enjoy its sharp acceleration and zippy feeling. But you have to stay mindful of the road while you're enjoying your new purchase. Don't be so busy pumping the pedals that you forget to slow down for a turn in the road. Don't pay so much attention to the feeling of a fresh spring breeze in your face that you forget about safe cycling in traffic. Don't forget that your traction is very bad on damp pavement. No matter how much you're enjoying yourself, you still have to stay alert and not go too fast for conditions, signal your intentions to other road users, and be ready to avoid their mistakes.

By following the maintenance schedules suggested in this book and by learning to ride in tune with road and traffic conditions, you can help ensure that your new bicycle will provide you with years of cycling enjoyment.

The Editors,
Bicycling magazine

Part One
General Maintenance

Precision Tune-Up

When the first sunny Saturday mornings of spring roll around, do you ever find yourself holed up in a dark, damp basement working on your bike, while all your friends are out riding and enjoying the day? What do they know that you don't?

They know that to enjoy riding in the spring, you have to get ready in the winter. This is especially important for those of us who live in the Snowbelt. After all, Sunbelt riders can use their bikes all year long, fixing small problems as they occur. But something happens to bikes put away in October. Parts rust. Cables unravel. Bolts loosen. It's an extraordinary phenomenon, this unceasing entropic movement by an otherwise inanimate object.

Though the cause of this deterioration may be mysterious, its remedies are not. Thus, we've put together a short guide to help you get your bicycle back in shape and ready for a long, trouble-free season after a period of disuse. The work won't take long; it's easy to do; and if you begin in December, you will be out of the basement when spring weather rolls around.

Cleaning and Waxing

Perhaps the best way to begin your reclaiming project is to clean and polish the bike until it sparkles. There are two reasons for this. First, it's easier to work on a clean bike; parts work better and hold their adjustments when clean. Second, it's easier to psych yourself up for the job if you clean the bike until it looks like new and then get all the running gear fixed up to match.

So get out a bucket of water, a soft sponge, some clean, soft cloths, and a little dishwashing detergent. Wipe off the accumulated grease first with a paper towel dipped in a solvent such as kerosene. Otherwise, it will simply smear all over the bike. Then, wash down the machine, top to bottom. Be sure to get it wet first before wiping it with the sudsy sponge, or the paint may be scratched. If the spokes are rusty or corroded, much of the accumulation can be removed with a small scrub brush. Rinse off the soapy water, but be careful not to aim the hose directly at any of the bearings (headset, hubs, crankset, or freewheel). Dry the bike with a soft towel.

Next, apply a coat of automobile wax to every surface except the braking surfaces of the rims. Some mechanics prefer to use a metal polish such as Simichrome on aluminum and chrome-plated parts, but a combination auto wax and cleaner (a wax with a small quantity of rubbing compound mixed in), such as Du Pont Rally or Simoniz SuperPoly, works just as well and eliminates the separate waxing operation. Waxes such as Rain Dance and Turtle Wax do not contain polishes and thus will not buff up the metal quite as well.

Wheels

As every cyclist knows, wheels are the most important parts on the bike. Clean, free-running, true wheels are a pleasure. Cranky, misaligned, wobbly wheels are not.

There are three parts to consider on the wheel: the hub and bearings, the spokes, and the rim. If any one of these is in questionable shape, consider replacing the part. Hubs and bearings generally last a long time; if they're gritty, but the races are in good shape, they can be cleaned and repacked. Rusty or broken spokes must be replaced, of course. Bent rims can sometimes be retrued, but you may need a wheel builder's advice here.

The most important thing is to make an honest appraisal of the wheels' condition. If you have steel rims, are they pitted, rusty, and bent? If they are, now is the perfect opportunity to replace them with aluminum equivalents. You'll get lighter wheels, better braking, and banish rust all at once. Aluminum rims are the best bargain in bicycling.

If the wheels are only in need of a little touch-up work, begin with the bearings. Clean and repack them, and replace any worn out cones or balls as necessary. Don't try to straighten a bent axle; replace it. Adjust the bearings before truing the rim. (Consult the separate chapter on hub maintenance for details on how to make these adjustments.)

If you're capable of overhauling the bearings, you can certainly learn to retrue the rim yourself. But, if you have doubts, take the wheel to your dealer or a local wheel builder (call a few bike clubs to locate a good one). True wheels are a joy forever—you won't regret the time you invest, if you work on them yourself, or the expense, if you have a professional create them for you.

Tires and Tubes

Some people recommend installing new tires and tubes at the start of every season, but the object of this may be mostly psychological. Seeing those glossy new boots on your spiffed-up rims makes you want to get out and ride. But tires last a long time; you can get as many as 5,000 miles out of nonracing versions. So if you've worn the old ones out the previous year, or if they're bald, cracked, or patched beyond recognition, replace them. Otherwise, just pump them up to make sure the tubes hold air for at least a few days at a time, and ride the tires until the tread wears out.

If you are a cyclist using sew-up tires, you have an added task. Peel the tubulars off, clean the rims, and reglue the tires. Don't start this season on last year's glue. Rolling a tire off the rim while rounding a corner is an experience you want to avoid.

Bearings

After the wheel hubs, the most dirt-sensitive and heavily loaded parts of a bike are the crankset, headset, and pedal bearings. If these haven't been overhauled recently—or if they were done so long ago you can't even remember when—it's best to begin from scratch. Disassemble, clean, inspect, regrease, reassemble, and readjust as necessary. (For details see the chapters on bottom bracket and headset maintenance. Once you have mastered those tasks, servicing pedal bearings should pose little difficulty.)

Chain

Bicycle chains, for all their complexity and numbers of parts, are ridiculously inexpensive. Thus, if the chain has a few seasons on it, is dry and rusty, worn, clanky, irredeemably dirty, or has sticky links, replace it.

Nonderailleur bike chains have master links; use a pair of pliers to squeeze off the master link clip, then pull the link apart. When you install the master link, make sure the open end of the clip faces opposite the direction of normal chain travel (when the link is on the top run of chain, the open end should face the rear).

Here's a trick you can borrow from dirt bikers to keep the chain clean: get a length of plastic tubing made for the purpose from a BMX shop and wrap it around the new chain. Be sure to glue the ends together following the manufacturer's instructions. This simple product will easily double the life of the chain by keeping dirt out and will reduce your maintenance chores.

Derailleur-geared bicycles can't use the plastic tubing, and their chains don't come apart as easily, either. You'll need a chain rivet extractor to disassemble them. These are available for three or four dollars and should be sold with a set of instructions.

If the old chain is in good shape, remove it and clean it thoroughly in a safe solvent such as kerosene. A toothbrush makes a fine scrubbing tool. Let the chain dry, then lubricate it with the juice of your choice: grease, paraffin, chain lube (sold in bicycle, BMX, or motorcycle shops), or petroleum distillates (such as WD-40, CRC, and the like). Paraffin has the advantage of being grit-free and has demonstrated the best antiwear characteristics. Melt it down in a double boiler and soak your clean chain in it for about five minutes. However, it doesn't really matter which lubricant you choose so long as you use it regularly and clean the chain whenever it seems to have accumulated more than its fair share of debris.

Cables and Casings

Another set of components better replaced than fussed with are cables. On a neglected bike, brake and gear cables are more likely to have rusted, either clear through or rust-welded to the cable casing, than to have frayed or snapped. If the cables look rusty, frayed, mangled, or kinked, replace them. Be sure to take the old cable with you to obtain the correct length, diameter (especially important with derailleur cables—fat Italian ones won't fit through skinny French lever ferrules), and cable end shape and size.

If the old cables are serviceable, remove them, coat them with waterproof grease, and slip them back into their casings. An alternative is to remove the cable at the brake or derailleur and drip a penetrating lubricant down the casing. This works, but not as well as grease.

Cracked, kinked, broken, or end-frayed casings should be replaced. Your dealer can cut new ones to the exact length you'll need. Bright transparent colors are now in vogue and really make a bike stand out. (No, they're not as cool as the old peppermint plastic wrap we put on the cables as kids, but they're still pretty sharp.)

Brakes

A quick romp down a congested city street with poorly adjusted, balky brakes is convincing evidence that a good set of brakes is second in importance only to the wheels. Fortunately, most brakes are reliable, strong, and indifferent to the elements.

The most troublesome caliper brake component is the cable, which you've already attended to. With that checked and adjusted, there is little else to worry about. Check the condition of the pads, of course, and make sure they meet the rims squarely.

Photograph 1–1. Once a year, check your brake and gear cables for rust and wear. If they remain serviceable, remove them from their housings and coat them with grease.

They should hit the rim at the same time, too, or nearly so; if not, center the brake, and on centerpulls (including cantilevers), make sure that the transverse cable stirrup is centered. If the brakes do not work smoothly, lubricate the caliper pivot points (be careful to keep lubricant off the pads and rims). If they are still stiff, perhaps the pivot bolts are too tight. A final cause might be a bent caliper arm. If so, replace the brake—don't straighten it.

Coaster brakes only need a few drops of oil a month to keep them working well. Also check the arm restraint at the chainstay for a tight connection.

Hub brakes should get the same cable attention as calipers. Also lubricate the pivot points and check the shoes. (The different types of brakes and their maintenance are discussed at great length later on in the book.)

Frame, Seatpost, Stem

Most people don't realize it, but frames, seatposts, and stems need lubrication, too. Without it, frames rust inside, and posts and stems seize in their mounts. So pull the post and stem and shoot some aerosol lubricant down the seat tube and through the holes into the top tube and down tube. Then rub a thin coat of grease on the parts of the seatpost and stem that fit into the bike. Antiseize compound is ideal for this job, by the way, so if you have some, use it instead of grease.

Slide the parts back into place, tighten their mounting bolts, and wipe off the accumulated grease. Here are two more tips: when you have adjusted these parts to their optimum positions, scribe or scratch a line on them where they meet the frame or headset. That way you'll know how far to insert them next time they are serviced. And don't tighten the bolts too tight; the parts should be free to move under the force of a hard blow (such as a crash) so that they don't break or bend the frame.

Finally, turn the bike upside down, remove the front wheel and front brake (except cantilevers), and stick a cork in the steerer tube. Cut the cork flush with the underside of the crown. Then drill through the brake mounting bolt hole and replace the brake. This simple plug will do your steerer tube and stem more good than anything else you can do for them. It's a small touch, but extremely worthwhile.

Bolts and Bodies

The next to last item on your maintenance list should be a round of general bolt tightening. Check the crankarm, chainwheel, brake, seatpost, and stem bolts. Make sure the pedals are tightly screwed in, and check that the brake lever clamps are tight on the handlebars.

You are now almost ready to ride. There's one more thing you can adjust—yourself. The start of a new season is a perfect time to look at your riding position and style and decide whether you're cycling as efficiently as you might. Check your leg extension reach and saddle position; look at the way your hands sit on the brake levers and in the drops. Are you comfortable? Does the bike feel like an extension of your body? If it does not, adjust your riding form until you and your bike are in sync, then go out and enjoy the best cycling season of your life.

Inflating Tires

Proper inflation of tires is important, and although it seems like an easy thing to do correctly, it is well worth your time to learn how to properly inflate a tire. Your bike will require less effort to pedal; it will feel livelier; and you'll be protecting yourself against annoying flats and expensive rim damage when you ride on properly inflated tires.

In most cases, you should inflate your tires to the pressure recommended on the tire sidewall. The challenge comes in learning how to get that amount of air pressure in your tire.

Check the pressure of your tires with a gauge to see how much pressure you need to add or subtract. This will give you an approximate idea of how many strokes with your pump you'll need. (A rough guideline: one stroke of a frame pump adds around one pound of pressure, depending on the size of your frame pump and the size of your tire. A floor pump takes about half as many strokes.)

Secure the pump's chuck onto the tire valve. If your tires have Presta valves (the less-familiar kind, which are generally found only on more expensive bikes and skinnier tires), you need to unscrew the small nut on the end of the valve so air can get into the inner tube. If you can't find a small nut on top of the valve, you undoubtedly have Schrader valves, which have no parts to loosen during inflation.

Keep in mind that different pump chucks secure onto tires in different ways. Most, but not all, Presta chucks have no locking mechanism. You simply shove the chuck onto the valve and rely on the rubber gasket inside the chuck to provide an airtight seal between the pump and the tire.

Most, but not all, Schrader chucks have some sort of locking lever. By looking at your pump and playing with it, you can figure out which lever position means "lock" and which means "unlock." Flip the lever to unlock, slip the chuck over your valve, and flip the lever to lock. Some Schrader chucks screw onto the valve stem.

Make sure that you're in the proper position to begin pumping. If you're using a floor pump, the hose from the pump to the tire valve must not approach the tire valve at a crooked

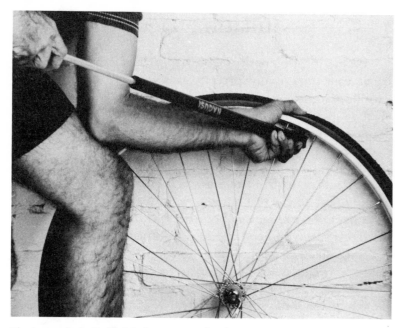

Photograph 1–2. Hold the pump chuck securely onto the valve and pump with a smooth, steady stroke.

angle, or the joint between the chuck and the valve will be strained, and air will leak out of that joint. Orient your pump and hose so that the joint isn't strained.

Pump steadily and evenly. Frame pumps and valves are fragile, so remember to make a smooth, steady effort. Don't flail wildly at the pump; concentrate your energy into smooth strokes.

Shortly after you've started pumping, stop and look to make sure your tire is properly seated on the rim. Closely inspect every inch of the line where the tire tucks under the rim's lip. Then inspect the other side of the rim. What you're looking for are bulges caused when the tire's bead isn't seated in the rim's bead seat. If you see a bulge, it will be obvious—the tire will be swollen around that point. Quickly deflate the tire and work the tire with your fingers to seat the bead on the rim. Inflate and try again.

Check the bead seat a couple more times during the course

Photograph 1–3. Presta valves have a small nut on the end that must be partially unscrewed to allow air into the tire.

of pumping your tire. When you estimate that you have the tire pressure you want, it's time to remove the pump. If your pump has a locking lever, you simply unlock the lever and pull the chuck off. If there is no locking lever, you just pull. Pull hard but smoothly and without any side-to-side jerking. If your pump chuck is screwed on, unscrew it as quickly as possible. Some air will escape while you're doing this. Try not to let the hissing noise bother you, just work as fast as you can.

Check your tire pressure with the gauge. If the pressure is satisfactory, you're ready to ride. If not, add or remove air as necessary.

One last caution: don't try to save time and use an air machine at a service station. Your bike tire does not hold enough air to enable you to carefully adjust the amount of incoming air. You may save a few minutes by using an air machine, but most likely, you'll pop the tube with too much air pressure.

How to Take Care of Your Bike— All Year Long

This maintenance schedule is designed to give you a handy reference for performing regular maintenance procedures. It is meant to be a guide, not a mandate. The amount of time you spend bicycling, the miles you travel, the road conditions, and the weather in your area will play major roles in determining the appropriate time lapse between maintenance jobs. Rain, dirt roads, and high temperatures are especially hard on a bike. Where these conditions are a significant factor, a more intense maintenance schedule should be pursued.

Some cyclists enjoy tinkering with their bikes and practice preventive maintenance at frequent intervals just for the fun of it. Others couldn't care less and do only what is absolutely necessary to keep them on the road. Thus, you should consider your own personal attitude, along with your riding habits and environmental factors, when deciding on a specific time sequence for performing needed maintenance tasks.

Expensive repairs usually become necessary as the result of simple neglect. In the long run, preventive maintenance saves you money. More important, it keeps your bicycle in safe operating condition and makes it easier to ride. Working on your own bike also helps you get better acquainted with your machine, thereby making you a more sensitive and more accomplished rider. However, if after considering these arguments, you still prefer not to do all of your own maintenance, use the chart to guide you in deciding when to take your bike to your local bike shop. Most shops are aware of special maintenance requirements in their own areas and give reliable service and advice.

Lubrication

The specific brand of lubrication you choose is a personal decision, but here are some guidelines.

Bearings: Greases are not all created equal. Pack your

14

bearings in a good-quality bicycle grease. Don't use oil with or instead of grease.

Derailleurs, freewheel body, brake pivot arms: Use lightweight machine or bicycle oil no heavier than 20-weight engine oil. Lightweight sprays penetrate well but do not leave sufficient residue. Apply oil only to the actual point of friction; spraying the entire component is wasteful and attracts dirt. Thoroughly clean the part first, then apply the oil, wiping off the excess. A hypodermic syringe or a needle applicator is an excellent means for applying the lubricant.

Chain: Everything from Yak fat to exotic space lubricants has its advocate. Commonly used substances include hot engine oil, liquid paraffin, spray chain lubricants, Teflon lubricants, and dry lubricants containing molybdenum disulfide. What you use is not as important as how you use it. The lubricant must penetrate the inner parts of the chain, resist friction and water, and should not attract dirt. The outer surface of the chain does not need lubricating, so whatever you use, be sure to wipe the outer portion of the chain to remove the excess.

Three-speed rear hubs: Use medium-weight bicycle oil or 20-weight engine oil.

Brake and derailleur housing: Spray the interior of the housing with lubricant, and grease the enclosed portion of cables, or run the cable over a block of paraffin several times. Teflon-lined cable housing and the enclosed cable should not be lubricated.

Maintenance Schedule

Every Ride

- Check tire pressure.
- Bounce bike and listen for rattles.
- Squeeze brake levers for adequate leverage.
- Make sure brake-release mechanism is in closed position.
- Check position of brake blocks on the rim.
- Check front and rear wheel quick-releases to make sure they are secure and that wheel is centered in frame.

- Spin each wheel to make sure nothing is catching in spokes.
- Look at condition of tires.
- Make sure bags and panniers are secure with no loose straps to catch in wheels.

Every Month (or more often if riding in rain)

- Wipe down entire bike with damp rag; look for cracks in frame, rims, and cranks.
- Check chain for dirt; oil or clean and lubricate stiff links as needed.
- Clean freewheel cluster with stiff paintbrush (one-inch) or rag.
- Clean chainwheels with rag.
- Lubricate interior of freewheel body.
- Check crankset bolts for tightness on cotterless and cottered cranks.
- Lubricate pivot points on front and rear derailleurs.
- Lubricate pivot points on brakes and levers if needed.
- Pinch pairs of spokes together to check tension; correct if needed.
- Check cables for kinks and fraying.
- Check wheels for trueness and dish; correct if necessary.
- Clean brake pads and rims with alcohol.
- Check rack bolts and all add-ons for tightness; don't overtighten.
- Check condition of glue holding tubulars to rims.
- Add two to four drops of oil to three-speed hubs.
- Clean leather saddles with saddle soap or dressing.
- Lubricate interior bushings of jockey and idler pulleys on rear derailleur.
- Check toe clips for cracks; dress toe straps.
- Check headset for proper alignment.

Every Six Months

- Check front and rear hubs for proper bearing adjustment.
- Check pedals for proper adjustment.
- Check bottom bracket for proper adjustment.

- Check chain, cogs, and chainwheel for wear; replace if worn.
- Check condition of brake blocks; replace if worn or hard.
- Apply rubber and vinyl preservative to gum rubber hoods and vinyl coverings on cable housings.

Every Year

- Overhaul pedals.
- Overhaul front and rear hubs.
- Overhaul headset.
- Overhaul bottom bracket.
- Remove brake and derailleur cables from housing; replace if worn or rusted; lubricate.
- Check frame alignment.
- Replace toe straps.

Part Two
Hub and Headset Maintenance

Overhauling Hubs

If you are just starting to perform your own bicycle maintenance, you will find overhauling hubs—disassembling, cleaning, and relubricating them—a necessary, but easy, job that will help prepare you for more demanding tasks. How often you overhaul your hubs should be determined by how much and what kind of riding you do—especially how much riding you do in the rain. For most cyclists, once or twice a year is often enough.

When is it time to overhaul your hubs? One way to tell is to remove a wheel from your bicycle and twiddle the axle between your fingers. If it feels gritty and tight or loose and sloppy, your overhaul time is past due.

But don't attempt to start the job until you have all the necessary tools at hand. This is important. No pair of pliers or adjustable wrench can take the place of cone wrenches or a freewheel remover, so trying to "make do" will only guarantee that you botch the job. Find a bike shop that cares enough about its customers to sell good-quality tools, and take your bike with you so you're sure you buy tools that fit it. Avoid cheap tools. Cheap cone wrenches, in particular, are annoyingly useless. Good ones will pay for themselves after just a few uses.

You will need the following tools:

- two cone wrenches to fit front hub cones (probably 13 or 14 millimeters—both of the same size)

- two cone wrenches for rear hub cones (probably 15 or 16 millimeters—both of the same size)
- a freewheel remover suitable for your particular brand of freewheel
- wrenches for the locknuts of both hubs (typically 14 to 16 millimeters front, 16 to 18 millimeters rear—metric open-end wrenches, cone wrenches, and small adjustable wrenches all work)
- a large adjustable wrench (12-inch handle) to remove the freewheel (use a securely mounted bench vise instead if you have one)
- tweezers or a small magnet to grasp ball bearings
- a small screwdriver
- a tube or can of good bicycle grease
- a small can of solvent
- rags
- an old toothbrush

Please note that our instructions relate to hubs found on derailleur bikes. Some 1-speed and 3-speed bikes have front hubs that can be overhauled without tools. Those hubs have one cone permanently fixed on the axle. The other cone screws on and off and has no locknut to hold it in place. Hubs of that type are easier to overhaul than the ones we'll describe.

Remove the Freewheel

The derailleur bike's rear hub is somewhat more complicated than the front hub, so we'll describe it first. After overhauling your rear hub, you will find working on your front hub to be a snap.

With the wheel removed from the bike, the first step is to remove the freewheel. (While it's possible to overhaul the hub with the freewheel in place, we don't recommend trying it.) Remove the quick-release skewer or axle nut and fit the freewheel tool's prongs or splines into the body of your freewheel. (If your freewheel tool has prongs and not splines, you should reinstall the skewer or axle nut to hold it onto the body. This is optional for splined freewheels because of their ample contact with the body of the tool.)

If you're using a wrench to remove your freewheel, hold the wheel on the floor and stand leaning over it. Fit the 12-inch adjustable wrench on the wrench flats of the freewheel remover so that the wrench handle is in the three o'clock position (if you are left-handed) or the nine o'clock position (if you are right-handed). Put one hand on top of the freewheel to hold it in place and the other hand on the wrench. Pause, take a deep breath, and focus your powers of concentration. If you are using your left hand, give a strong pull upward on the wrench while holding the freewheel absolutely still. If you are using your right hand to apply the pressure, push down hard. In either case, the freewheel should begin to unscrew in the conventional, counterclockwise direction.

If you're using a vise, removing the freewheel is somewhat easier. Just clamp the freewheel remover in the vise, grab the rim on either side, pause, and give a sharp counterclockwise

Photograph 2–1. If you don't have a bench vise, a freewheel can be removed using a large adjustable wrench.

twist. As soon as the freewheel breaks loose, stop. Remove the quick-release (or axle nut) and then spin the freewheel off the hub. You now have easy access to both sides of your rear hub.

Remove the Axle

Now it's time to remove the axle so you can get at the bearings. To do this, simply unscrew one cone and locknut and pull the axle out of the hub. But before you begin, keep the following two things in mind.

First, the job is easier if you leave one cone/locknut set tightened on the axle. If you don't, you'll have to fuss around when you reassemble the hub so that just enough axle protrudes beyond the locknuts on each side. With quick-release hubs, you have very little margin for error in this adjustment. The wheel won't go on the bike properly if the axle protrudes too far on one side and not far enough on the other. So leave one cone alone.

Second, on the rear hub, the cone you should remove is the left cone. Why? Cones are screwed onto the axle with ordinary right-hand threads. If a left cone loosens, it will unscrew slightly. The locknut will stop it from loosening further, and you'll have a very slightly loose bearing. But if the right (freewheel side) cone comes loose, it will screw into the bearings and cause them to bind, damaging the hub. Since you have to remove the freewheel to adjust the right cone, now's a good time to put one wrench on the right cone, another on the right locknut, and tighten them against each other severely. Make sure they won't come loose.

To remove the axle, put a cone wrench on the left cone and another wrench on the left locknut. Holding the cone wrench still, loosen (turn counterclockwise) the locknut. It should unscrew and come off the axle.

In between the locknut and cone is a key washer, which has a little tang that fits into the slot on the axle. The idea is that the key washer can't rotate, so you can turn the locknut without the cone turning. But the tang usually gets stripped off, so don't count on the key washer to work. (Don't discard it, however; the axle is built with its width in mind.) You may need to pry the key washer loose with a screwdriver before it will slide off. Once it is removed, you're ready to unscrew the cone.

When you unscrew the cone, it's possible to suffer the unwanted chaos of ball bearings raining all over the floor. There's an easy way to avoid this. Set the wheel horizontally on the workbench or floor, cluster-side down. The weight of the wheel will hold the axle in place so the cluster-side bearings can't fall out. Now unscrew the left-side cone and remove it. Grab the wheel in one hand and the axle in the other. Lift the wheel off the floor and let the axle drop down halfway inside the hub to allow access to the left-side bearings. The axle will still trap the right-side bearings in place.

Count the left-side bearings. Use fingers, magnet, or tweezers to get all the left-side bearings out. Count them again and set them in a container. Now drop the axle clear of the hub and collect the right-side bearings in another container. If you want, you can use a screwdriver to pry the dust caps (little metal washer-shaped pieces) loose from the hub. This makes getting at the bearings easier. If you do so, be careful—it's easy to bend a dust cap.

Clean the Bearings

Put the ball bearings on a rag and wipe off as much grease as possible. Then move them to a clean rag, bundle them up securely, and agitate the rag with the bearings in a small can of solvent. If you can't find solvent in small enough quantities (try gas stations and hardware stores), use paint thinner, kerosene, or home heating oil (the latter two will work, even though they leave a greasy film). When the bearings are clean, open the rag and inspect each bearing individually. If you find any with flat spots, dents, cracks, or dull spots, it is best to replace the entire set. They are cheap and easily available at your neighborhood bike shop. Most front hubs use 3/16-inch balls; most rear hubs, 1/4-inch balls. But there are exceptions, and you should take some old bearings along to match the size.

Next, clean all grease and dirt from the hub's bearing cups. When clean, inspect them for any major pits or rough spots.

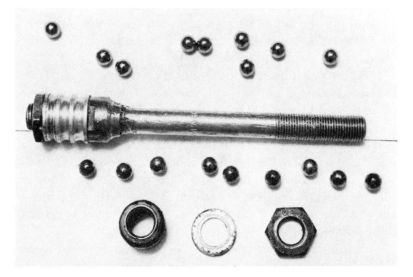

Photograph 2–2. When overhauling a hub, leave the cone, washer, and locknut in place on one end of the axle to simplify reassembly.

On some hubs, the ball cups are replaceable, but such parts are very hard to find so the job should be delegated to your bike shop mechanic.

The axle, cones, key washers, and locknuts can now be cleaned by dipping them in solvent and wiping with a clean rag. Carefully inspect the cones for pits and rough spots, indicating a need for replacement. See if the tang on the loose key washer is intact. If it isn't, you might want to see if you can buy a new one. Check the axle for stripped threads while cleaning the threads with a stiff toothbrush. Check for a bent axle by replacing the left cone and observing how the axle rolls on a flat surface such as glass. If it is bent, you will need a new one.

In most cases, you won't need to replace any parts. Bicycle parts generally last a long time if they receive regular maintenance.

Lubricate the Hub

You are now ready to lubricate and reassemble the hub but, first, a word about grease. Buy a high-quality grease formulated for bicycles. If the grease you buy does not come in a tube with a long nozzle, you might want to purchase a large (4 to 6-inch) plastic hypodermic syringe without the needle. (Syringes are available at feed and farm stores.) Get one with a ½- to 1-inch tip. This is a handy tool for inserting grease into tight spots during various maintenance projects.

Begin to reassemble the hub by applying a generous amount of grease around the inside of both bearing cups. Place the ball bearings into the greased cups. (A tweezer comes in handy for this.) There should be a space about the size of one bearing left when all the bearings are in place. You may find an improper number of bearings in a new hub, so don't rule out adding or subtracting some. Almost all rear hubs use nine balls per side; most front hubs use ten.

If you removed the dust caps, replace them (with their sharp edges down) and use a hammer to gently tap them flush with the hub. Carefully insert the axle into the freewheel side of the hub. Screw the left cone back into position "finger tight" (don't use a wrench). Drop the key washer down the axle against the cone, then screw the locknut in place.

Now is the time to adjust the cones against the ball bearings. This is a crucial step, so don't rush it. On quick-release wheels, you should adjust the cones and tighten the locknut so that a barely detectable amount of play can be felt when push/pulling the axle. This disappears or is barely discernible at the rim when the wheel is held in place with the quick-release, because the quick-release skewer compresses the axle. On wheels with axle nuts, you should adjust the cones so that there is no play but no binding either.

Remember, the cone is held in place by the locknut. So use a cone wrench to get the cone in the proper position, then use another wrench (cone wrench, adjustable wrench, or open-end metric wrench) to tighten the locknut against it. The best approach is to slightly overtighten the cone and then loosen it.

This is why you want to have the luxury of two cone wrenches instead of one. You can loosen the left cone by putting a wrench on its locknut and another on the cone itself, but it's sometimes hard to get the exact adjustment you want. The failsafe way to get the proper adjustment is to overtighten the cone, snug the locknut against it, and then put a wrench on each of the two cones. Twist slightly to loosen them with respect

Photograph 2–3. Use a pair of cone wrenches to make the final adjustments on your hub cones.

to each other. You'll find it easy to get the adjustment right, and both locknuts will be snug. If you only have one cone wrench, the job will be more difficult, but keep at it, and you'll get it right.

Clean the freewheel threads and grease them liberally. (This grease is important for future freewheel removals.) Replace your spoke protector, if you wish, and carefully screw the freewheel onto the hub. Be sure it goes on straight with no cross threading. Replace your quick-release skewer and the springs that center it on the axle, and you're ready to put the wheel back on the bicycle.

After doing the rear hub, the front is simple because there is no freewheel, chain, or derailleur to contend with. As with most bike repair projects, overhauling your hubs will probably take longer than you expect, the first or second time, but after getting a little experience under your belt, the job will go quite fast. Anyway, no matter how long it takes you, the feeling of accomplishment and the joy of smooth-spinning hubs are well worth the time and effort. Try it, and you will be well on your way to competence in bicycle maintenance.

Miles Ahead: Headset Care and Maintenance

Quite often, the headset of a bicycle is not only ignored but forgotten. Some recent books on bicycles and bicycle components don't even mention headsets, and those that do fail to explain the headset's function and care.

The headset is not a large and obvious part of the bicycle like the crankset. It does not have a sophisticated movement like the derailleurs, but it does a job that can affect the handling of the bicycle more than any other component. The performance of even the finest custom frame can be jeopardized by the improper installation, adjustment, or maintenance of the headset.

First, let's look at what a headset does. It supports the front fork in the bicycle frame. The headset holds the fork still, preventing side-to-side and forward-and-back movement. At the same time, the headset allows the fork to rotate about the axis of the steering column. The headset must withstand the massive pressures transmitted from the road through the fork without adversely affecting the handling characteristics of the bicycle.

Servicing a Headset

Not all headsets can be serviced. Some sealed types and some of the more exotic plastic models are serviceable only by replacement. Since they cannot be opened for inspection, failure comes as a complete surprise. You cannot look for and correct problems (pits, chips, cracks, etc.) in the early stages. Once these headsets fail, your only recourse for repair is the nearest mailbox, assuming that the manufacturer's address is known and that he can rebuild it. Moreover, since none of the exotic designs are free from flaws, we strongly prefer the conventional, user-serviceable headsets. Virtually all new bicycles have them, and replacement parts for them are generally available.

If you have a conventional headset on your bike, the instructions that follow will enable you to overhaul it. A glance at the number of steps involved indicates that there is no quick, simple way to complete the job. The headset must be disassem-

27

bled, cleaned, inspected, reassembled, and adjusted. It's a good project for a rainy Saturday, so don't be put off by it. Here's what to do.

1. Disconnect the front brake cable, no matter whether the brake is sidepull or centerpull.

2. Remove the handlebar and stem as a unit. Loosen the stem bolt slightly (some have an Allen head, some a conventional hex head). Place a block of wood on top of the bolt head and rap it once smartly with a hammer. This will dislodge the expander wedge in the stem. If the stem is still tight, loosen the

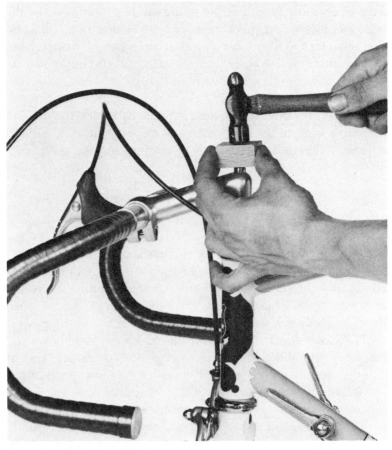

Photograph 2–4. Place a block of wood on top of the stem bolt and rap it smartly with a hammer to dislodge the stem expander wedge.

bolt another turn and rap it again, repeating the process until the stem is loose. Slip the stem and bars out of the fork.

3. Remove the front wheel. If you plan to replace the fork crown race (see following points), remove the brake from the fork.

4. Loosen and remove the locknut by unscrewing it counterclockwise, using a wrench of the correct size. Special headset spanners work best, but for this application, a 12-inch adjustable wrench is okay. However, Shimano EX headsets require special tools. Conventional headset spanners will bridge the flats on them, so you might think they'd work fine, but because of the limited contact area, the tools will chew up the soft aluminum. If you have one of these Shimano headsets, either buy the correct tools or let a bicycle dealer service it. Never use locking pliers, slip-joint pliers, or other serrated-jaw tools on any headset because they will scar the finish and can deform the components.

5. Lift off the brake cable hanger, if your bike has centerpull brakes, and the lock washer.

6. Support the fork from underneath so it can't fall and let the bearings escape. Unscrew the adjusting race. Do this carefully in case the bearing balls inside are loose (not held in a cage). If the balls are loose, some will stick to the race and some to the fixed cup as you lift off the race. Retrieve and save them. (A dropcloth on the floor will help slow down any balls that fall.)

You should always replace used balls with new ones. The old ones will have developed flat spots, and proper adjustment will be impossible if they're reused. But the old balls, whether loose or caged, should be saved; you'll need to know their size and number when buying replacements. Most conventional headsets use $5/32$-inch bearing balls; some use $3/16$-inch balls; and a few use $1/8$-inch balls. The only way to be sure is to read the information with your headset or measure the balls.

7. At this point, the fork is free to be lowered out of the frame. But since the lower race may have loose balls (even if the upper race didn't), take precautions: hold the fork and frame together, turn the frame upside down, and raise the fork out of the frame. This way, most of the balls will sit in the cup-shaped, lower pressed race. Set the fork aside, and scoop the balls out of the race. Count the number of balls because many headsets use different numbers on the top and bottom.

8. It is not necessary to remove the pressed races or fork crown race for an overhaul. They may be cleaned on the frame and fork. Clean all the associated parts with a safe solvent such as kerosene.

If the fork crown race is to be removed, the best way is to use a hammer and a special U-shaped punch that can drive the crown race off without damaging the fork. Improvised tools,

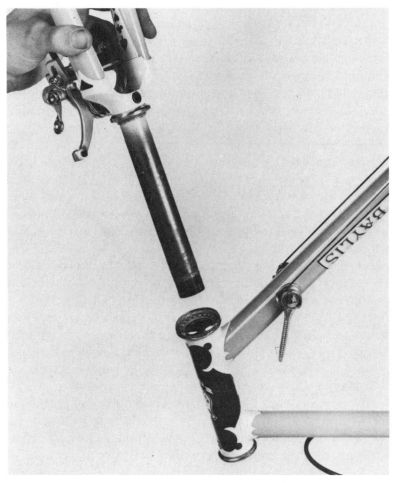

Photograph 2–5. To avoid losing bearings from the lower race, turn the frame upside down while removing or installing the fork.

such as vises and blocks of wood, may damage the fork or warp the crown race. For the pressed head races in the frame, there is a special punch with four flared sections. Use a hammer with the punch to drive these races out. A hammer and long drift punch can also be used, but these tools make the job go slower, and they may damage the head tube if they're used improperly. Since special tools are required to replace the pressed components, do not remove them unless absolutely necessary.

9. Inspect the races for pits or cracks. Replace any components that show signs of excessive wear. Replace the components with the same brand and model part. Mixing is not advisable since the result may not work correctly.

10. Special tools are also required to reset pressed races. These tools are expensive and not found in most home mechanics' tool chests so get help from a bicycle shop to reset these pressed headset components. The shop will use a special slide hammer to reset the fork crown race. For the head tube races, there are special presses, which do the job very well and assure that the races are put in straight.

11. Reassemble the headset by applying a moderately thick coating of grease to the bearing balls for the lower stack. Replace the balls on the fork crown race. If they are loose balls, heavily grease the fork crown race and stick the proper number of balls to the race. If the balls are caged, remember to put the cage in properly. (A ball cage resembles a C in cross section.) The area between the two curved-in points—the "open" side of the cage—should be turned down toward the ground so that the cups will fit around the closed side.

12. Now grease the upper pressed race and the bearing balls. If the balls are caged, put them in the race, making sure the race is turned in the proper direction, as explained above. If the balls are loose, be sure to use enough grease to hold them in place.

13. Grease the threads of the steering column—or better yet, use antiseize compound. (It is available from auto parts stores.) Also grease the entire steering column to prevent corrosion. Grease the adjusting race bearing surface. Now slide the fork into the frame and thread the adjusting race down until it contacts the upper bearing set. Do not overtighten, or the headset will be damaged.

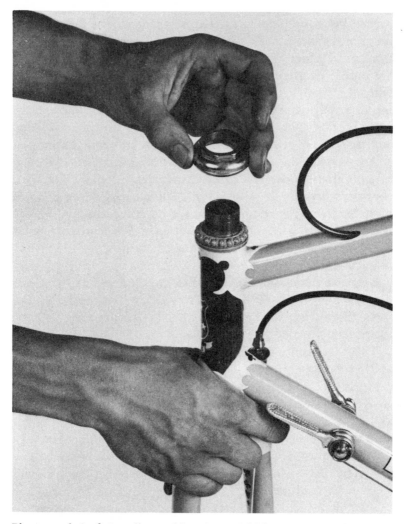

Photograph 2–6. Install caged bearings with their "open" side against the conical bearing contact area. Then fit the adjustable cup over the "closed" side.

14. Slide on the lock washer and the brake cable hanger (if present). Thread on the locknut.

15. Adjust and lock down the headset using wrenches of the correct size. Many companies make headset adjustment tools, and they are a good investment. Ordinary wrenches will slip easily, so if you use them, be careful. You may wish to purchase a small clip (the 712/3 tool) made by Campagnolo. It fits around the lock washer and helps prevent the other tools being used from slipping.

Here's an important tip that most mechanics don't know: when adjusting the headset, do not overtighten and then back off to find the correct adjustment. This common practice will perform an impromptu Brinell hardness test on your headset and most likely ruin it. The compression will dent your races, and the headset will wear out prematurely.

To adjust the headset properly, tighten the adjusting race slowly, preferably by hand, until it contacts the bearings. Back off a tiny bit to compensate for the compression the locknut will add. Hold the adjusting race stationary while tightening the locknut. Insert the stem and handlebars and tighten the stem bolt. Check for any play or looseness. If loose, tighten the adjusting race some more. Retighten everything and check again.

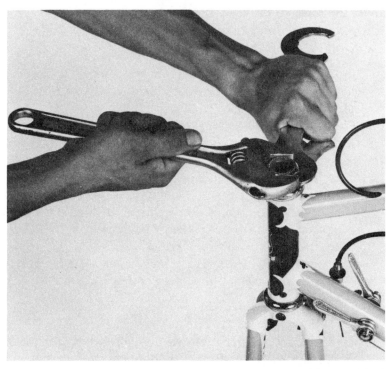

Photograph 2–7. Use wrenches of the correct size to adjust and lock down the headset. Make final adjustments after installing the stem.

The stem should be tightened into the steerer tube while adjusting the headset because it will affect the final adjustment. (If the handlebars make it difficult to adjust the headset, you can use an old stem with no handlebars to make the final adjustment.) And before you insert the stem for the final time, give it a coat of antiseize compound or grease so it won't seize in the steering column.

Troubleshooting

When checking a headset, make sure that there is no back-and-forth or side-to-side motion. Check the fork when it is in several different positions. Recheck it once the bicycle is fully assembled. Lock the front brake and rock the bicycle back and forth while it is on the floor. If you hear a clicking noise or feel any play, the headset must be readjusted. Any looseness will allow the forks to oscillate in the frame on downhill runs and when braking, so proper adjustment is vitally important.

Suppose you find that the fork binds?

1. If using loose balls, make sure you have not used too many. (To be sure they aren't overcrowded, fill the race and then subtract one or two.)
2. If using caged balls, make sure the cage is inserted correctly.
3. Check for a bent fork causing misalignment. Bent forks must be replaced. See your bike shop.
4. Make sure the stem is installed before adjustment is made.
5. See if the steering column is bent, preventing proper alignment of the races. A bike shop or frame builder may be able to replace it; it cannot be reliably straightened.
6. Make sure the balls are the correct size.
7. Make sure all the pressed races have been seated properly.
8. Make sure you haven't mixed old and new parts.

What if the forks are too loose?

1. Make sure the steerer tube has enough threads for the adjusting race to come all the way down.
2. If loose balls are used, make sure there are enough.

3. Make sure all the parts are for the same headset.
4. Check to see whether the lip on the locknut is too thick, preventing the locknut from seating against the lock washer. If this is the problem, use an extra lock washer.

Loose vs. Caged Bearing Balls

Many people want to replace their caged bearing balls with loose ones because more balls can be squeezed into the upper and lower race. "The more bearings, the better the load distribution," is their logic. This is okay for most headsets, and it is often the only option for less expensive headsets (since replacement cages may not be available). However, the better quality caged bearings are almost as good as loose bearings and are certainly easier to assemble and disassemble.

If you do opt for loose balls, note that top-quality headsets come with balls in matched sets, all within a small tolerance (Campagnolo bearings are within 0.001 millimeter of each other, for example). Do not throw in one strange ball since it will probably have an adverse effect on your headset adjustment.

Service

How often does a headset require service? This question is difficult to answer because everyone's riding habits are different. Road surface, rider weight, weather, and the amount of dirt in the air all affect the condition of the headset. Watch the buildup of road soot on your front brake and the lower stack of your headset. This will give you an indication of the amount of dirt you are encountering.

As a general rule, we recommend that a headset be cleaned and adjusted at least once a year. Damaged components should be replaced whenever the forks bind or develop notches that prevent free movement. When replacing components, always use plenty of grease and be sure to adjust the headset properly.

Extra Protection

Other than the maintenance procedures already described, there is not a lot that can be done to protect a headset. However, one additional thing that heavy-weather riders can do is put a "boot" over the upper and lower stack to prevent dirt and water from penetrating. It is more important to protect the lower stack than the upper since more of the road soot collects there. A boot is an elastic cover that prevents anything from penetrating the headset and contaminating the grease in the bearings. Usually, you make a boot by cutting a one-inch section out of an old inner tube. It is best to use a black butyl rubber tube because white natural latex tubes break down quickly from air pollution and sunlight.

Several years ago there was a commercially produced boot available that had to be inserted during the installation of a headset because it fit under the fork crown race. You may wish to check with your local bike dealer to see if he sells such a device. None of the dealers with whom we spoke have heard of such a product, so chances are you will have to make your own. It is especially important that you protect your headset bearings when carrying your bike on a car roof rack. Otherwise, the high-speed winds will blow the grease right out of your bearing races. In this case, you can simply wrap both the upper and lower stack with plastic wrap or duct tape to get the needed protection. For road use, boots made from inner tubes are preferable to tape or plastic because they will add less drag to the rotation of the steerer tube.

Part Three
Bottom Bracket Maintenance

Cottered Crank Removal

If your bicycle has a three-piece crankset, as most do, the first step in overhauling your bottom bracket is to remove the crankarms from the ends of the bottom bracket spindle. But there are two types of three-piece cranks, cottered and cotterless, and the method for removing their arms is not the same.

Cottered cranks are the older technology. They're usually found on fairly inexpensive bicycles, but many older bicycles of top quality also have them. They can be quite satisfactory in use but are harder to work on than the newer cotterless cranks. There is a special tool, called a cotter press, which is made for installing and removing cotters. However, this is strictly a shop tool; it weighs several pounds and is quite expensive. Bicycle shops that do a great deal of work on cottered bottom brackets might consider investing in a cotter press; the tool does the job quite satisfactorily. However, for the individual bike owner/mechanic, a less expensive tool is needed.

Several alternatives are available. Two that have been suggested at various times in the pages of *Bicycling* magazine are (1) a heavy-duty C-clamp used with a short piece of steel pipe to receive the emerging pin and (2) a large Vise-Grip. These tools are used like the cotter press to apply a gradual but steady force on cotter pins to either break them free for removal or properly seat them during installation. Rather than go into more detail about these methods at this point, we want to focus our attention on the most common technique used to remove cotters—hammering them out.

A cotter pin that has been properly installed can be driven out of its crankarm by one or two very hard hammer blows. This can be tricky because unless you take careful aim, you can severely damage other parts of your bike. Because of the fear of missing, a common mistake is to attempt to remove a cotter by tapping very lightly on its threaded end. After a few light taps, you'll realize the cotter pin hasn't budged, and more forceful blows will be necessary to achieve significant results.

But after a few more vigorous blows with the hammer, you will probably see the threaded end of the cotter begin to resemble a mushroom, and you will realize it will never accept a nut again! Some experts will tell you to loosen the nut but leave it on so that if the threads are damaged, unscrewing the nut will correct the damage. This is fine in theory, but in practice there is usually not enough length on the threaded end of the cotter to do this. Other experts will recommend that you put a block of wood over the cotter's end so the hammer blows won't damage the threads. But the cushioning effect of the wood also blunts the full force of the hammer; a solidly packed cotter just won't give when struck in this way. So what can you do?

Concentration Is the Key

The key to successfully removing cotters with a hammer is to take careful aim so you won't need more than one or two sharp blows to do the job right. This is easier said than done, but it is a skill that can be learned with a little practice. It calls for the type of concentration shown by karate experts. A karate-trained board-breaker is taught to form a mental picture of the board with the hand going right through it before attempting the blow. In the same way, you should try to picture your hammer coming down into the cotter and going right through, breaking off the end of the spindle in the process. It won't, but this fantasy may help you to use the strength of your arm fully.

The truth of the matter is you don't need particularly strong arms to hammer out a cotter. What you need is the willingness to effectively use the strength you have. To really do the job right calls for deadly accuracy and a certain amount of barbaric abandon. In the tradition of the oriental martial arts, you need to concentrate and channel your energy into one or two effective moves. Make your hammer "go with the flow," and you will see the stubborn pin "go at the blow."

Picking the Right Hammer

It always helps, of course, to pick the right tool for the job at hand. The three most common types of hammers are the claw, ball peen, and sledge. The sledge hammer has a curved face that won't drive cotters out squarely and is, in any case, too heavy for this job. The ball peen, the head of which has a wedge or hemispherical end opposite the face, is generally regarded as a metalworking tool and would seem to be the logical choice. However, in our experience a 16- or 20-ounce claw hammer (carpenter's hammer) is better than either the ball peen or sledge in removing cotters. A claw hammer usually has a more nearly flat striking surface, and its face is angled advantageously for removing cotters.

Absorbing the Impact

When hammering on cotters, there's always a chance the impact of the hammer blows could damage the bearings in the bottom bracket. You can prevent this by supporting the crank from below while you are hammering. One way is by holding the head of a sledge hammer underneath the thick end of the crank so that the mass of the sledge hammer will absorb the impact. This works but is a bit awkward to do without assistance.

A better way to support the end of the crank is to use a short length of pipe, braced between the floor and the underside of the crank at the bottom bracket. This transfers the impact directly to the floor. (If you care about your floor, put a strong block of wood under the pipe.) The pipe surrounds the end of the cotter, leaving room for the cotter to move, but it gives excellent support to the end of the axle. A more traditional variation on this type of support is a block of 4 × 4 lumber notched at one end to provide space for the pin to exit the crankarm. The length of pipe or wooden block needed depends on how the bicycle is being held—for example, whether it is standing on both wheels or suspended from a stand.

If you have a professional-type stand that clamps onto your bike's seat tube, you can adjust the height of the bicycle by choosing where to grip the seat tube. With such a stand you can use a single length of pipe for many different frame sizes. Otherwise you will have to cut the pipe to fit the distance between your axle spindle and the floor when your bike is standing on its wheels. A good choice of pipe to use is ¾-inch cast-iron gas pipe. (Note that pipe is usually measured by the inside diameter, unlike bicycle tubing.) The diameter of pipe is

Photograph 3–1. Place an appropriate length of pipe between the crankarm and the floor to absorb the shock of the hammer blow on the cotter pin.

not really critical; we suggest this size because a scrap piece of it can usually be acquired for a token sum from a shop that specializes in plumbing and heating.

Welcome Back, Cotter

If you have both skill and luck working for you, the cotter will fly out on your first or second blow. If not, you're in for trouble. After a few blows, the threads of the cotter will be ruined, but the cotter may still be in tight. After a few more good smacks, the threaded end of the cotter will probably bend away from you. If you are using a claw hammer, the claws are the perfect tool to pry the cotter straight again. If it is a really tough one, you may hammer and bend it until the threaded end breaks off. Then it's time to get serious!

Since the pin will no longer be protruding from the crank, you will need to use a drift punch that can go into the cotter hole to drive out the remains of the cotter. If you don't wish to buy one, a good punch for this purpose can be fashioned out of an old pedal spindle by grinding the thin end flat. These spindles are made from the same superior kind of steel used in good tools. They are thick at the end you hit, but they taper nicely to a size that will fit into the cotter hole of the crank.

Do not try to hold the punch in your hand because, if you miss, you could do yourself a serious injury. Even if you don't miss, the closeness of your hand will inhibit you from hitting the punch as hard as you must. The punch should be held with a pair of pliers, preferably locking pliers such as a Vise-Grip.

When All Else Fails

Once you have resorted to a punch, 95 percent of cotters should come out without need for more heroic measures. If yours is among the 5 percent that still won't budge, there are two more things to try. One is to drill the cotter out. Use about a ¼-inch drill bit and plenty of oil. Drill all the way through the cotter lengthwise. In most cases, this will relieve enough pressure that the remains of the cotter can be easily driven out with a punch.

If that fails (and we have never known it to fail), your second option is to heat the crank with a propane torch. This expands the crank, including the hole that the cotter is in. Once the crank is well heated, the cotter will come out easily with a punch. This measure is used as a last resort since overheating the crank will weaken it. Do not heat the crank so hot that it changes color, much less becomes red-hot.

Replacing Cotters

Unless you have succeeded in removing your cotters without causing them any visible damage, plan on replacing them. They are not very expensive, and it is not worth using defective cotters that will only give you trouble at a later time. However, cotter replacement may create some problems because of lack of standardization. Usually, all cotters made in a given country will be of the same diameter, but there is very little standardization of their flat faces, either their angle or their depth. If possible, try to obtain replacement cotters made or distributed by the manufacturer of your bicycle.

To reassemble your crankset, the cotters must be hammered in just as they were hammered out. If you try to tighten them just by tightening the nuts, you will not be able to get the pins in tight enough and may strip their threads. Hammer the cotters, then snug down the nuts. Hammer a bit more, then tighten the nuts again, until further hammering does not produce any more slack. After 50 miles or so of riding, give the cotters a couple of taps and tighten the nuts again. After that they should be secure.

An Alternative Technique

If you have qualms about the heroic use of hammer and punch on cotter pins, you may wish to adopt an alternative method for removing and replacing your cottered cranks. Your principal option is to replace the sharp blow of a hammer with strong, steady pressure from a vise type of tool such as the commercially produced cotter pin press. A homemade alternative to the expensive commercial tool is a heavy-duty C-clamp. Place a short length of steel tubing over the head of the pin to provide a path for its exit, then fit the clamp over the tail of the pin and the end of the tube. Use a heavy wrench to tighten the clamp against the pin, forcing it out. A variation on this technique involves the use of a large pair of locking pliers, such as those made famous by Vise-Grip, in place of the C-clamp.

When using the pliers, you must adjust them to provide maximum tension on the cotter pin once you squeeze them into the locked position. Leave them on the pin for an hour or so, then remove them and adjust them for heavier tension before fitting them on the pin again. Do this as many times as necessary until the pin breaks free. You may eliminate the need for the short piece of tubing by fitting one jaw of the pliers over the tail of the pin and the other on the crankarm beside the head of the pin. But be sure to aim the pin in a direction where it will do no harm when it comes flying out of the crank. New pins may be installed with these tools by applying pressure on their heads rather than their tails.

Overhaul Your Bottom Bracket

The bottom bracket of your bicycle is an important component assembly that requires periodic maintenance. The crank spindle, bearings, and cups fit into it, and the crankarms, chainwheels, and pedals are extensions of it. How often you overhaul the bottom bracket depends on the amount and type of riding you do, but an average recommended service interval is one year. If you ride in the rain or in sandy areas, it should be overhauled every six months or less. Preventive maintenance

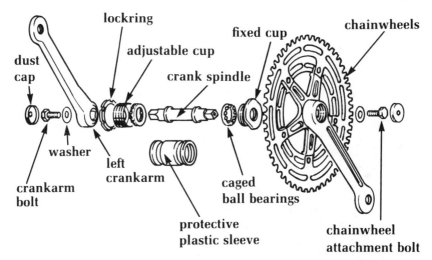

Illustration 3–1. An exploded view of a cotterless crank, bottom bracket assembly.

extends the life of your bottom bracket assembly and eliminates costly replacement of parts.

To overhaul the bottom bracket, first study Illustration 3–1, which depicts the component parts of a bottom bracket that employs a cotterless crankset. Memorize the name of each part and develop a clear picture of how the parts relate to each other, then gather the necessary tools and equipment in your work area. (The instructions that follow assume you are working on a crankset of this type. If your bike has a cottered or one-piece steel crankset, you will need to modify the tool list and procedure somewhat.)

Here is what you will need.

- Allen wrench or wide-blade screwdriver to remove dust caps
- crankarm bolt spanner or socket wrench for removing crankarm fixing bolts
- crank puller to remove crankarms from the axle
- C-spanner for loosening the bottom bracket lockring
- pin spanner or an ordinary wrench for removing the adjustable cup
- magnet or tweezers to handle the ball bearings

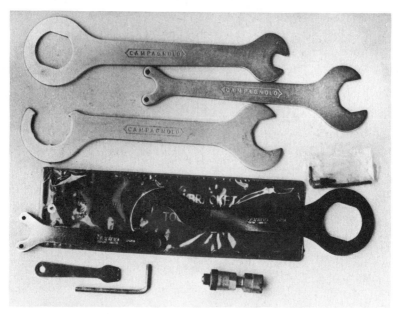

Photograph 3–2. A collection of bottom bracket tools.

- toothbrush to clean threads
- good-quality bicycle grease
- cleaning solvent to clean parts
- rags for cleaning hands and parts
- Blue Loctite or other anaerobic adhesive to secure cups
- protective plastic sleeve (if your bicycle doesn't already have one)

When purchasing tools, take your bike with you to the bike shop, or if ordering by mail, know the brand name and model of your crankset to be sure of getting the right tools.

The overhaul procedure is easier if you use a chain rivet tool to break a link so you can remove the chain completely from your bike. While it is off, you can also clean and lubricate it. If you don't want to take the chain off completely, then move it inside the chainwheels and take up the slack at the rear of your bike to keep it out of your way while you work. Now you are ready to begin disassembling your bottom bracket.

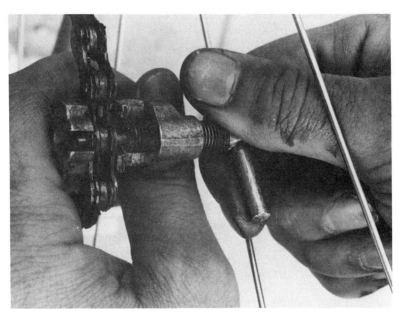

Photograph 3–3. Breaking a link of chain or rejoining a broken link can be quickly and easily accomplished with a chain rivet tool.

Remove the Crankarms

First, remove the dust caps (if any) from the crankarms. The most common types either have a six-sided hole, which requires a five-millimeter Allen wrench, or a long slot into which you can fit a coin or wide-blade screwdriver. (Your crankarm bolt spanner may also have an appendage made to fit dust caps.) Turn each cap counterclockwise carefully since they are soft and easily damaged.

Once the dust caps are removed, you have access to either bolt heads or nuts that hold the crankarms to the crank axle. Crank bolts can be 14, 15, or 16 millimeters. If you are substituting a thin-walled socket for a crankarm bolt spanner, be sure to get a good fit, then turn the nuts or bolts counterclockwise until they are free.

The crankarms will still be stuck on the slightly tapered spindle ends so you will need a crankarm puller to remove them. Be absolutely certain that you buy the right puller because

Photograph 3–4. An Allen wrench is the only tool needed to remove this type of cotterless crankarm.

threads on crankarms differ, and irreversible damage results if the wrong tool is used. Screw the puller clockwise all the way into one crankarm's female threads. Then, turn the puller's threaded plunger clockwise to push it against the end of the spindle while the body of the tool pulls the crankarm free. (Unless your puller has an attached handle, you will need a socket or adjustable wrench for this.) Repeat the process with the other crankarm. If you ever have to pull a crankarm with stripped threads, you can do it with a machinist's gear puller (available at hardware stores).

Take this opportunity to thoroughly clean the chainwheels attached to the right crankarm. Use a toothbrush and a rag dampened in solvent, or if they are really dirty, soak the whole unit in solvent. This is also a good time to check for tightness in the chainwheel fixing bolts. Replacements for these bolts are very difficult to find so it is prudent to tighten them to make sure they won't fall out. Some mechanics use anaerobic adhesive on the threads of these bolts to prevent them from coming loose. That's an excellent idea if you only use a tiny bit. However, too much anaerobic adhesive will make the bolts unremovable, forcing you to drill them out someday. A tiny drop will accomplish what you want.

Disassemble the Spindle and Bearings

After you've removed both crankarms, you can disassemble the bottom bracket bearings and spindle. Start by loosening (turning counterclockwise) the lockring on the adjustable cup, found on the left side of the bottom bracket. This requires a special wrench called a C-spanner or simply a spanner wrench. This tool has a semicircular end with a small projecting tab. The semicircle wraps around the lockring, and the tab hooks into one of the notches cut into the lockring's outer edge. All bottom bracket lockrings are similar in size, though some have fairly small notches. Make sure the radius of the "C" on your spanner is nearly the same as that of your lockring and that its tab will fit into your lockring's notches.

Once the lockring is off, the adjustable cup can be removed by turning it counterclockwise. Some adjustable cups have a small hexagonal projection that can be grasped with a wrench, preferably one made to fit it. Most adjustable cups have small holes drilled into them to receive another specialized tool called a pin spanner. Spanners with pins fixed a set distance apart will fit only one or two brands of cups. Models with movable jaws and replaceable pins are more versatile.

Before you take out the adjustable cup, prepare to catch and count all your ball bearings. Many bicycles have caged ball bearings, which are easy to deal with, but don't count on it. Unless you know otherwise, assume your bike has loose balls.

Spread newspapers on the floor or workbench. Put the bicycle on its side, adjustable cup down. With one hand, hold the top of the crank spindle. (When it's held in place, balls from the fixed cup are trapped in place.) With the other hand, finish unscrewing the adjustable cup. Some bearings will come out with the adjustable cup; others will be caked with grease and stuck to the spindle, waiting for you to pluck them loose. Put all the bearings in a common container for cleaning.

While you fish with your fingers, tweezers, or magnet for the extra bearings, do not yield to the temptation to turn the bike frame upside down. That will allow bearings to roll downhill into the frame tubes where you'll have an awful time retrieving them.

When all adjustable cup bearings are out and accounted

for, lower the spindle out of the bottom bracket. Some fixed cup bearings will rain onto your newspaper; others will need to be fished for. Note that the fixed cup end of the spindle is about ten millimeters longer than the adjustable cup end to provide clearance for the chainwheels. Remember this when you begin reassembling the bottom bracket.

With a rag or paper towel, remove as much grease as possible from the adjustable cup, spindle, bearings, and (by reaching inside the frame) the fixed cup. Soak the rest of the grease off by submerging the parts in a can of solvent.

After cleaning all traces of grease and dirt from the components, check each one for irregular wear, cracks, or pitting. If any ball bearings show irregularities, replace both sets of caged bearings or the entire set of loose ones. Replacements are inexpensive and are available at local bike shops. Take your old bearings along to match the size. Use a stiff toothbrush to clean the threads on the adjustable cup and the bottom bracket itself, then inspect them also. Check both the adjustable cup and the fixed cup; if either has deep pits, is out-of-round, or has deep grooves, both cups should be replaced.

Removing the fixed cup is a poor idea unless you have a good reason for doing so—for example, if you need to replace it. It's not meant to be removed very often. But if you must remove it, check first to find out which way it is threaded. The fixed cup on English-threaded bottom brackets has left-hand thread (turn clockwise to loosen); whereas, the fixed cup on French- and Italian-threaded bottom brackets has right-hand (conventional) thread. However, many French bikes sold in the United States have English bottom bracket threads so it is a good idea to check.

If your fixed cup has wrench flats, you can clamp the flats in a sturdy bench vise and unscrew the frame from the cup. (Yes, it's screwed in mighty tight.) If your fixed cup doesn't have wrench flats or if you have trouble with the bench vise technique, take the bike to a shop that has the special spanners (some cost more than $100) to remove the fixed cup safely. Before replacing the fixed cup, clean it and its threads thoroughly. Also clean the threads in the bottom bracket and make sure the two sets of threads properly match. Tighten the cup securely in place before greasing it.

How to Reassemble

Reassemble the bottom bracket in the following manner.

1. Pack both cups with light-viscosity grease. (Some heavier greases, such as automotive axle grease, are too thick for this job.)
2. If your bearings are caged, pack grease around the balls before installing the cages in place.
3. Nestle the bearings, whether caged or loose, in their races in the greased cups. If they're caged, they must be installed in a particular way. In cross section, a bearing cage is shaped like a C. Install the cage so that the open side of the C is turned inward, away from the cup.
4. Lightly grease the bearing races on the spindle.
5. Insert the spindle into the bottom bracket, long end first. Press its bearing race against the fixed-cup balls and give it a few twists to make sure it turns smoothly.
6. If your bike does not have a plastic protective sleeve covering the bearings and crank spindle, buy one (or make one out of a plastic milk bottle) and install it at this time. It helps keep dirt and water out of the bearings. Slip the sleeve over the spindle and bearings on the fixed cup.
7. Screw the adjustable cup (with the bearings held in place by grease) into the bottom bracket. Continue screwing until it is finger tight. If you have had trouble with the adjustable cup and/or lockring coming loose, a few drops of anaerobic adhesive on the threads may help.
8. Screw on the lockring.

You're now ready to adjust the bearings. Use the appropriate tool (pin spanner or wrench) to turn the adjustable cup until the spindle just starts to bind in its bearings. Now use the C-spanner to tighten the lockring. If the adjustable cup turns with the lockring, it will end up too tight. In this case, loosen the cup and lockring together, then back the lockring off a bit in relation to the cup before retightening them both together. If the adjustable cup does not tend to turn with the lockring, then tightening the ring may actually loosen the cup a bit. In either case, it may take you several tries before getting the adjustment just right. After tightening the lockring each time, twirl the spindle. It should not bind at all, though it may run a bit stiff. Some stiffness is to be expected; only the most expensive cranksets can be adjusted to eliminate extra looseness without leaving any stiffness in the spindle.

Obviously, the difference between stiffness and binding is highly subjective, but you should be able to feel it. If your bearings are binding, loosen the lockring, then twist the cup ever so slightly. Tighten the lockring and check the adjustment again. If the bearings are still too tight or loose, repeat the procedure. Be patient. It may take a half-dozen attempts, but you should be able to adjust your bearings to exactly the right degree of tightness.

Now you're ready to install the right (chainwheel side) crankarm. (If you put the spindle in backwards, you'll soon find out—the chainwheels will scrape the chainstays.) Do not lubricate the tapers on the crank spindle or the inside of the crankarm.

Place the crankarm on the spindle. Hold a heavy hammer or other solid object against the opposite end of the spindle while using a rubber, leather, or wooden mallet to strike the crankarm directly over the end of the spindle. This seats the crankarm in position. Grease the threads and, with the washer in place, screw the nut or bolt onto the spindle. Use your crankarm bolt spanner or socket wrench to tighten it firmly. Use the crankarm to double-check for free play in the spindle bearings. You'll find it harder to detect binding in the bearings with the crankarm in place.

Install the left crankarm as you did the right. Then check to see that your crankset spins smoothly. To seal the bottom bracket bearings against dirt and water, wrap a pipe cleaner around each side of the spindle next to the bearing cups. Even better, wrap it with heavy cotton twine. (This also works on hub bearings and is very effective.) Replace both dust caps. Replace the chain.

Each 50 miles for the first 150 or 200 miles, check the tightness of the nut or bolt that holds the crankarm onto the spindle. This is important. If the crankarms work loose, their female tapers will quickly be ruined—an expensive mess. Check for free play in the bearing adjustment periodically; readjust the bearings, if necessary.

There you have it. A clean, well-adjusted, and lubricated bottom bracket assembly lasts for thousands of miles, and you will enjoy the feeling of accomplishment and pride from having done the work yourself.

Part Four
Gear and Brake Maintenance

For Better Shifting—Tune Up Your Rear Derailleur

Is your rear derailleur hard to shift? Even if you've cleaned and lubricated the chain, does it shift past the gear you want to the next one? If so, chances are the rear derailleur is in need of adjustment. Making sure the chain is the correct length, positioning the rear wheel properly in the dropouts, and a few other simple adjustments can often dramatically improve a derailleur's performance. Also, a rear derailleur shifts best if its upper pulley is fairly close to the cogs. Different types of rear derailleurs use different means to position the upper pulley; we will discuss the various types and explain how to adjust them.

There are three main types of rear derailleurs, which we will call the Campagnolo Record type, the SunTour GT type, and the Simplex/Shimano type.

Campagnolo Record Type

Both the body and the upper pulley above the chain cage pivot on Campagnolo Record derailleurs have fixed positions. As large cogs and chainwheels take up more chain, the upper pulley moves backward and down around the chain cage pivot. Many other derailleur manufacturers have copied this chain cage design, which dates back to when Campagnolo invented the world's first parallelogram-action derailleur. Some of the brands that use this style are Zeus, Mavic, Galli, Ofmega, Gipiemme, and Gian Robert.

Campy Record–type derailleurs work most consistently with chainwheels only a few teeth apart in size. The design was developed in an era when racers used 49/52 chainwheels; today's 10-tooth and 12-tooth gaps between chainwheels sometimes cause the jockey pulley on these derailleurs to swing far away from the cogs when you make a front shift. The resulting increased distance between the jockey pulley and the rear cogs can lead to poor shifting. Also, the largest cog you are supposed

Photograph 4–1. Rear derailleurs of the Campagnolo Record–type work best when your freewheel cluster contains no oversized cogs and your chainwheels are only a few teeth apart in size.

to be able to use with a Campy Record derailleur has 26 teeth. However, we have heard of one pushed to 31 teeth with 47/52 chainwheels. The exact limit depends on the length of the dropout hanger. (Dropout hanger differences are discussed at the end of this chapter.)

Despite the limitations of the design, if you adjust your chain length carefully, it is often possible to use Campy Record–type derailleurs with a wide step between chainwheels and with oversize cogs. Adjust the chain so that when it is on the largest cog and large chainwheel, the derailleur's upper pulley is rotated back and down. Then try the setup on a test stand before applying foot power.

With the chain on the largest cog, try shifting back and forth from the small to large chainwheel. Then do the same with the chain on the smallest cog. If the derailleur threatens to bend when you attempt the cross-chain combinations (small-large and large-small), either switch to another derailleur or lengthen the chain. But if the only problem is that these shifts hang up, you can live with it since you shouldn't use the cross-chain combinations in your normal gear sequence.

If you do not already have a rear derailleur of this type and expect to be using chainwheels separated by a wide step and oversize cogs, you would be better off to select a derailleur of a different type. There are good-quality derailleurs available on the market today suited to every need. It really makes no sense to try to force one type to serve every purpose.

SunTour GT Type

The angle of the SunTour GT at the dropout hanger is fixed; the body of the derailleur does not spring fore and aft when you shift. Also, the GT's upper pulley is in line with (concentric with) the chain cage pivot. Consequently, the upper pulley's position is not affected by the chain length. Though they look very different, most Huret derailleurs, except the Duopar, are of the same concentric-upper-pulley, fixed-body type as the SunTour GT. Since derailleurs come in different models for freewheels of different sizes, the best model to use is one whose upper pulley will ride as close to the cogs as possible without interference.

SunTour GT derailleurs have an angle-adjusting screw to allow additional freedom in setting the pulley-cog distance. SunTour recommends that you set the parallelogram mechanism parallel to the chainstay. If that setting does not give you the shifting precision you desire, you can use the angle-adjusting screw to raise the upper pulley closer to the cogs. The most precise shifting will probably occur when there is only about ¾ inch of straight chain between the pulley and the closest cog. Adjusted this way, a wide-range, concentric-pulley derailleur (for example the VGT) is the best type to use with a wide-range crankset when the cogs at the rear are small. This type of derailleur is unaffected by large differences in chainwheel size.

As a general rule, rear derailleurs work best with a relatively short chain. The shorter the chain, the less the weight that has to be moved around by the shift lever. A shorter chain provides more spring tension and snappier upshifting. Of course, there are limits; your chain must be long enough to make the shift to the large chainwheel when you're on the largest rear cog and short enough not to fall slack in the small-small combination.

A good way to select chain length is to start with the maximum chain possible without slack in the small-chainwheel/small-cog combination. Test your derailleur performance that way. If it is too sloppy, you can always take a link or two out of the chain. Remember, it is always easier to remove links than to have to add them.

Other considerations may affect your final choice of chain length. For example, SunTour GT–type derailleurs have a wide flange on the outer cage plate next to the upper pulley. Sometimes, when the chain is on the inside sprocket, this flange will hit the next sprocket. One way to eliminate the interference is to adjust the length of your chain. However, a better solution is to move the position of the derailleur by turning the body adjustment screw.

SunTour derailleurs that use the fixed-stop/raised-pulley mechanism (including models V, Vx, AG, and Cyclone) have tooth capacities that vary from model to model. Don't let the slant parallelogram fool you into thinking that all SunTour derailleurs work the same. Because of the raised upper pulley, the short-cage SunTour models (and the long-cage AG) have more in common with the Campy Record than with the SunTour GT derailleurs.

Simplex/Shimano Type

Most Simplex and Shimano rear derailleurs and the Campagnolo Rally have a sprung upper pivot. You can identify a Simplex/Shimano–type derailleur by trying to rotate the parallelogram mechanism forward with your hand. If it can be rotated fore and aft around the dropout hanger, it is of the Simplex/Shimano type. If it will not move forward from its normal working position, it is of another type.

Simplex and Shimano derailleurs use two opposing forces generated by their two springs to try to make the upper pulley "track" the sprockets regardless of their size. The spring in the pivot at the dropout hanger tries to pull the derailleur to the rear, away from the cogs. The spring in the chain cage pivot tries to rotate the upper pulley—located behind this pivot— upward into the cogs. When everything is in good adjustment, the forces of the two springs balance out to hold the upper pulley close to the cog in use, whether large or small.

The Huret Duopar uses a different arrangement—one spring acting on two parallelograms—to achieve a similar result. SunTour's new Tech series derailleurs also use a principle similar to that of the Duopar but with two springs. All of these derailleurs are especially good when a wide-range freewheel has small jumps at the top end—for example, a 13–14–16–19–24–32 6-speed. Other derailleurs will shift sloppily on the small cogs of such a freewheel because the large inner cogs require the upper pulley to be too far away from the small cogs. The self-adjusting upper pulley of the Shimano/Simplex/Duopar–type derailleurs can get closer to those small cogs.

Adjust these derailleurs by experiment. Start with the chain rather long; in the small-cog/large-chainwheel combination (top gear), the lower pulley of the derailleur's chain cage should be only slightly forward of the upper one. Keeping the chain on the largest chainwheel, shift across all of the cogs to see how well the upper pulley "tracks." If you pull forward on the lower

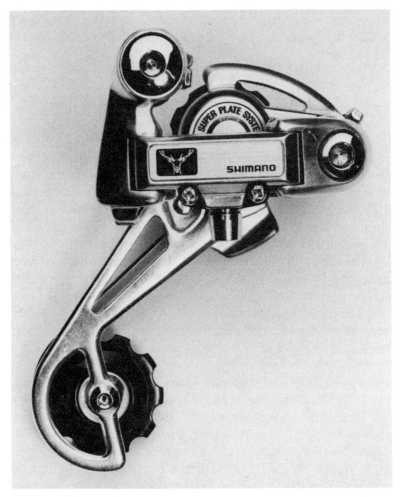

Photograph 4–2. The long, enclosed cage and sealed pivot bushings on this Shimano Super Plate make it suitable for use on all-terrain bikes.

run of the chain with one hand while keeping the cranks from turning with the other, you can see how shortening the chain would affect the "tracking."

Check performance using the smaller chainwheels, too. You may have to shorten the chain so it won't go slack in small-small combinations. But don't bother making it short enough for combinations you won't use, such as the outer cog with a triple crankset's "granny" chainwheel. No damage will occur from the chain's hanging slack if you shift to one of these combinations by mistake. When you have completed your experimentation, adjust the chain length to give the best overall "tracking."

Axle Position in the Dropouts

If your bike has the customary dropouts with horizontal slots and axle stops, axle position can be adjusted. If the derailleur is operating near its limit on a large cog, you may have to move the axle forward or back (usually forward) to gain clearance. Otherwise, use axle position to improve shifting.

Most derailleurs work well with the axle near the middle of the dropout slots. This gives the closest cog-pulley clearance consistent with adequate chain wrap on the smaller cogs. Adequate chain wrap decreases chain and cog wear and reduces the chances of the chain's slipping or jumping off during a shift. Generally, chain wrap should be 120 degrees or more on the smallest sprocket.

Simplex/Shimano/Duopar–type derailleurs are the big exception. Most of these shift more precisely with the axle forward in the slots. The spring-loaded "tracking" of these derailleurs pushes the upper pulley toward the cogs, also assuring adequate chain wrap—more nearly 180 degrees than 120—on these derailleurs. But if the axle is too far back in the dropouts, the upper pulley will flop up in front of the cogs. The length of chain between the pulley and cogs will be increased instead of decreased, and chain tension will be reduced. Shifting on the smaller cogs with this type of derailleur can become very sloppy if you let this happen and is especially good if you don't let it happen.

Dropout Hanger Differences

Considerable differences exist among different brands of derailleur mounting hangers. If the hanger on your bike is part of the right rear dropout, it may restrict your choice of derailleurs.

Old Simplex hangers have a 9-millimeter unthreaded hole. Most other brands use a 10 × 1-millimeter thread; Campagnolo uses 10-millimeter × 26 threads per inch (tpi). In practice, these two 10-millimeter threadings are so close to one another that derailleurs can be interchanged. However, don't change back and forth repeatedly because this will heavily damage the threads. And, if possible, before making the change, use a tap to recut the threads in the dropout hanger to fit the new threading precisely. Also, the old Simplex unthreaded hole can be threaded to allow the installation of derailleurs of other brands.

The length of the hangers varies, too. For example, Simplex hangers are long and Campagnolo hangers short; for this reason, a Campagnolo derailleur may shift sloppily on small cogs when installed on a Simplex dropout. Also, the limit on size of the largest cog of a derailleur is affected by the dropout hanger length. SunTour makes hangers of different lengths. You can use them to adjust the capacity of your bike to accept cogs of different sizes.

The position of the derailleur mounting hole varies with different hangers; it is farther forward in some and farther back in others. Altering the mounting hole location has the same effect as moving the axle forward or back in the dropouts. The stop that sets the angle of the derailleur may also be in different positions on different hangers. Some hangers have no angle stop at all. Huret dropouts have a stop that works only with Huret derailleurs, and the stop on Campagnolo dropouts slips past a SunTour₁ angle-adjusting screw if this is loosened to raise the derailleur close to the sprockets.

The most significant potential for problems exists when you must use a derailleur on a dropout of a different brand with a built-in hanger. But, on the other hand, you may gain an advantage by using the new derailleur, both because it may inherently perform better and because a shorter or longer hanger may actually work better with a particular set of cogs. In short, a lot of variables help determine the performance of your rear derailleur, and a lot of options are open to you in altering that performance.

Basic Derailleur Checkup

Before you try to test out the various adjustment refinements that we have been describing, ask yourself whether something more basic might be causing your particular derailleur problems. Check to make certain your gear cables are in good condition. Also, wiggle the derailleur to make sure its pivots aren't loose and check to see if they are well lubricated. Then get behind the bike and make sure that the derailleur isn't bent. A surprising number of cyclists ride with their rear derailleurs bent inward, the result of their bikes' having fallen on their right sides. If a bent derailleur is in good enough shape that it works at all, replacement is rarely necessary. Usually, it can be straightened by pulling it back out to its original position.

When straightening a bent derailleur, first check to see where it is bent. Look at it from behind. If the chain cage is tilted inward, then the dropout hanger is probably bent; this is the most common part to be bent. But also check the chain cage. Shift to a small chainwheel and small cog combination so the chain cage sticks out behind. Look down from above and see whether the chain cage points straight back in a line with the cogs or angles off to one side. If it's askew, it is probably bent. In rare cases, the dropout hanger is intentionally bent to angle the chain cage this way. You can check this by looking from above to see whether the chain cage pivot is parallel to the rear wheel's axle. If it is, the cage is bent; if not, the dropout hanger is bent.

Work carefully in straightening a bent derailleur. If only the dropout hanger is bent, then all you need to do is pull out

Photograph 4–3. Use an Allen wrench in the hex hole of the derailleur's upper pivot as a lever to straighten a bent dropout tab.

on it. There is a neat trick that will let you accomplish this
without even getting your hands dirty. Stick a six-millimeter
Allen wrench into the hex hole in the derailleur's upper pivot
and use this as a lever. In any case, don't pull on the chain cage.
You might bend it and complicate your job. If the chain cage

Photograph 4–4. Adjust your rear derailleur so that the chain runs
through the chain cage in line with the cogs in all gear combinations.

is bent, be careful to straighten it without bending any other part. Sometimes, it is easiest to remove the chain cage side plates and straighten them in a vise or simply to replace the derailleur.

Your goal in these adjustments is to make the chain run through the chain cage in line with the cogs in all gear combinations and to make the pivots work freely. After straightening, check the alignment once again by looking both from behind and from above in chainwheel/cog combinations that place the chain cage in both horizontal and vertical positions.

Be sure to readjust the high-gear and low-gear limit stops after straightening a derailleur. They will be affected by the changes you have made, and there is a risk of unshipping the chain if you overlook this step. Once you've completed these basic adjustments and repairs, if you are still dissatisfied with the performance of your rear derailleur, experiment with some of the more subtle adjustments discussed in the earlier sections of this chapter.

Know Your Brakes

The brakes are the most important safety-related components on your bicycle. If your brakes don't work well, you have to ride slower much of the time to compensate. Many cyclists pay this penalty, but if you learn how to maintain your brakes properly, you won't have to.

How Your Brakes Work

Most bicycles are equipped with caliper brakes, which consist of three parts: the hand levers on the handlebars, the caliper units (arms) that squeeze the wheel rims with rubber blocks, and the cables that connect the levers to the calipers.

The cables are the most misunderstood components and the ones that cause the most mechanical trouble. Each cable consists of two parts. The inner wire is thin, multistranded, and made of steel. It has a molded-on metal fitting at its lever end. This fitting is used to attach the cable to the lever. The other part, the housing, is a tube of steel, wound spirally like a spring. It is usually covered with plastic to prevent it from rusting and to keep the cable from scratching the bicycle's paint. The inner wire and the housing are equally important; neither works without the other.

The brake lever on the handlebars also has two parts: the movable part, which is the lever itself, and the stationary part, the hood, which attaches to the handlebars. The fitting at the end of the cable's inner wire attaches to the movable lever; squeezing the lever pulls on the inner wire. The cable housing attaches to the hood.

There are two common types of brake calipers: sidepull and centerpull. If the cable runs to the side of the caliper, you have a sidepull brake, and if the cable runs to the center, you have a centerpull.

Sidepull calipers work just like a pair of pliers, except that the "handle" ends are off to one side instead of being in line with the grabbing end. The "handle" ends are where the cable attaches. At the end of the upper arm is a fitting called a cable housing stop. This pea-size fitting has a small hole at the bottom of a larger hole. The inner wire fits easily through the small hole, but the housing cannot. The larger hole serves as a socket for the housing. When the brake is applied, the housing pushes down on the cable housing stop and moves the upper arm downward. The lower arm has a small pinch bolt at its end; this is the cable anchor bolt. A small hole runs crosswise through this bolt, just big enough so the inner wire can be threaded through it. When the anchor bolt is tightened with its nut, the inner wire is pinched and locked securely in place. When the brake is applied, the inner wire pulls up and applies pressure to the far side of the rim.

Many people believe that sidepull brakes work unevenly, pushing the rim to one side. This is not true since the housing pushes one arm just as hard as the inner wire pulls the other. On a mixte frame (a frame that has no top tube but two long tubes extending from the top of the head tube to the rear fork ends) whose rear brake cable comes up to the brake from below, the positions of the anchor bolt and socket are reversed between the two brake arms, but this makes no difference in the way the brake works.

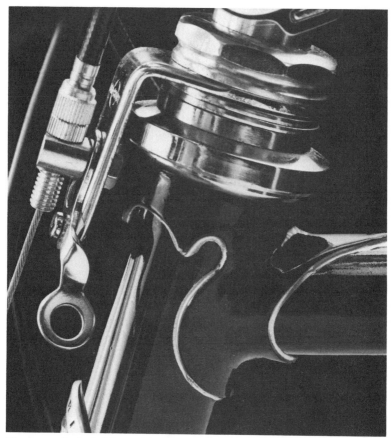

Photograph 4–5. The cable housing on a centerpull brake usually is attached to the headset.

Centerpull brakes, on the other hand, work somewhat differently. The cable housing stop does not attach directly to the caliper. It is a *fulcrum,* which is usually attached to the headset for the front brake and to the seatpost binder bolt for the rear brake. The two arms of the centerpull caliper are joined together by a *transverse cable.* The inner wire is hooked to the transverse cable by a piece called the *yoke.* An anchor bolt in the yoke clamps the end of the inner wire.

When you squeeze the lever, it pulls on the inner wire. The inner wire pulls up on the transverse cable, and this in turn pulls up on the ends of the two brake arms. Since the housing and the bridge of the caliper unit both attach to the frame, the push part of the push/pull action goes through the frame (or fork).

Either centerpull or sidepull brakes can, if properly adjusted, provide good performance for most riders. Sidepull brakes usually have a lower mechanical advantage; that is, less lever travel and a corresponding greater human effort moves the brake shoes the same distance. Consequently, sidepull brakes feel stiffer through the levers. But since the levers don't have to travel as far to move the shoes, this type of brake is easier to apply and release quickly.

Because of their quickness and the fact that they are slightly lighter, sidepull brakes are usually the first choice of bicycle racers. But the higher mechanical advantage of centerpull brakes makes them more powerful, if properly adjusted. Heavy people, cyclists carrying heavy touring baggage or pulling trailers, and people with weak hands often find that centerpull brakes serve them better. Still, be aware that a sidepull brake with good rubber pads will provide you with more powerful braking than a centerpull brake with poor pads.

Other types of rim brakes are the Shimano Parapul brake and the cantilever brake. These are both varieties of centerpull brakes. The Parapul brake uses a wedge to push the two brake arms apart at the top, instead of the usual transverse cable and yoke. The cantilever brake works in much the same way as the conventional centerpull brake, except that the brake arm pivots are attached directly to the frame or fork. Cantilever brakes are especially powerful and will be discussed in more detail later in the chapter.

Cable Maintenance

Whatever type of brakes you have, if your brakes are properly adjusted but still work poorly, cable friction is most likely the cause. In extreme cases, this will keep your brakes from releasing when you let go of the levers—you might have to push the levers back out. Even when friction is less severe, it still can use up a significant part of your strength, decreasing the power of your brakes.

Excessive friction is often caused by kinks in the brake cables. If you turn a bicycle with dropped handlebars upside

Photograph 4–6. Brake cable housing should arch over the handlebars as low as possible without kinking. Excess length should be cut away.

down while making repairs, the weight of the bicycle will rest on the cables just above the brake levers, kinking them. So when you work on your bike, hang it up or use a repair stand. Kinking is also often caused by sloppy routing of cable around baskets that attach to the handlebars. The cable should run in smooth curves with no unnecessary sharp bends.

You should also be aware that cables supplied on many new bikes are far longer than required; they are made to fit the largest bikes. The new housing should be cut very short. It should arch as low as possible over the handlebars without kinking, and there should be no unnecessary loop of cable over the rear brake. Needless curves and length add to friction.

Often excessive friction is caused by inadequate lubrication. Once a year, loosen the anchor bolts, pull the inner wires out of the housings, and coat them with grease. If instead of using good bicycle grease, you use medium-weight oil, be prepared to lubricate them again in a few months. Lightweight spray oils will only be good for a week or two. So use good grease, and the job will only need to be repeated annually.

Sometimes excessive friction is the result of incorrect cutting of the housing. If it is cut carelessly, the tail end of the steel spiral may curve inward and block the opening, rubbing on the inner wire. If the housing is cut correctly, the opening will be round. For a professional job, file the end of the housing flat after cutting it.

Ordinary wire cutters tend to smash a brake cable while cutting it. By contrast, special brake-cable cutting pliers grip the inner wire from four sides to cut it cleanly. Unless you have the special pliers, take your bike and either the old cable or its measurement to a bike shop to have the new cable and housing pre-cut.

If you purchase universal brake cables rather than cables made specifically for your model of brakes, note that they are generally sold with a mushroom-shaped fitting on one end and a barrel-shaped fitting on the other. You should cut off one of these ends, retaining the end that fits your levers. Have the housing cut to the correct length, but leave the inner wire a little long to be on the safe side. You can have it trimmed later, any time you ride by the bike shop.

Since the rear brake cable on a mixte frame bicycle comes up from below, rainwater can fall down into the housing. If you have this type of brake, drip some medium-weight oil into the end of the housing every few weeks to displace water and prevent rust.

It is best to have a couple of spare cables on hand at all times. Carry one with you on long trips. If a cable on your bike has a broken strand or is kinked, it should be replaced immediately. Look up inside the brake lever to check for broken strands. Occasionally, a molded lever-end fitting will pull loose from an inner wire. This usually happens without warning, when you are braking. That's one good reason why your bike has two brakes and why you should carry a spare cable.

To replace a cable, loosen the anchor bolt, then pull the housing up and away from the brake lever. The inner wire will pull out of the brake and housing. Detach the cable from the lever. At the lever, there may be a ferrule—a metal or plastic socket for the housing—that comes off with the cable. Save this.

Grease the new inner wire (or the old one, if you are reusing it) and thread it through the lever. There will be a special slot or cone-shaped hole to receive the fitting molded on the wire's end. On most 10-speed bikes with dropped handlebars and appropriate brake levers, this slot or hole will be in a small cylindrical metal piece inside the lever.

Thread the inner wire through the special slot or hole and snag the fitting in the slot or hole. Double-check this step. Make sure the cable end is securely snagged. You may have to rotate the cylindrical metal piece to bring the slot or hole into proper position. Then thread the cable on through the hole in the top of the hood, through the ferrule (if there is one), and into the housing. Pull the end of the inner wire out the far end of the housing and thread it through the cable housing stop.

An old inner wire or a poorly cut or carelessly threaded one may fray at the brake end. This makes it impossible to thread the cable through the housing. Most new bicycles are supplied with little aluminum caps over the ends of the inner wires to prevent fraying, but you must remove these when you need them most—when you thread the cables. Sometimes you can twist the strands back together neatly, but often you can't. If the cable was extra-long originally, you can trim the inner wire and the housing by equal amounts (snipping off the frayed portion of the inner wire) and reuse them, but be sure to remove the inner wire from the housing before cutting the housing. If the housing has been kinked at one end, trim that end.

There is a good way to prevent fraying. After installing a new cable for the first time, clean the grease off its end. You'll usually need only a rag to clean the cable, but occasionally a chlorinated degreaser solvent, such as carburetor cleaner will be necessary. Then coat or "tin" the end with rosin-core electrical solder and a small soldering iron. The solder will hold the strands together so they cannot fray. Note—this only works on new cables because the plating on the individual strands wears off when cables age. Solder adheres only to this plating, not to the actual steel. (And it does not adhere to the stainless steel woven cable sometimes used on derailleurs.) The process we've described may sound like a hassle, but it's truly worth the effort; the results are wonderfully neat and clean.

Your brake should have an adjusting barrel either on the brake itself or on the hand levers. If it is on the brake, thread the inner wire through it and on through the anchor bolt. Tighten the nut; first get it just barely snug, then use pliers to pull the cable down through it to set the adjustment. Finally, tighten the nut the rest of the way.

It is very important that you tighten the anchor bolt just the right amount. In a panic stop, you squeeze harder than usual. If the anchor bolt is not tight enough, the cable can pull loose just when you need your brakes the most.

The anchor bolt is rather small and has a hole drilled in it, so it is not very strong. All experienced bicycle mechanics have learned how much they can tighten this bolt without breaking it. They learned by breaking a few when they were just starting. After you have broken a couple, your hand will know the limit. If you never break one, you are probably not tightening them enough. Lubricate the anchor bolt's nut with light machine oil; it will be easier to tighten, and the feel will be more consistent.

A good test of anchor bolt tightness is to squeeze each brake lever with both hands. If you can't pull the cable loose with both hands, you certainly will not be able to with one hand.

Brake Cable Adjustment

Determining the right cable length is the single most important factor in adjusting your brakes. If the inner wire is too long or the housing too short, the brake will be too loose and won't provide much stopping power. If, on the other hand, the inner wire is too short or the housing is too long, the brakes will drag on the rim all the time, making the bike very hard to pedal. So it is important to find the right cable length before tightening the anchor bolt.

There are two ways to adjust the cable length: a coarse

adjustment and a fine adjustment. To make the coarse adjustment, you need three hands: one hand to hold the brake shoes tightly against the rim (there is a spring that tries to push them away), one hand to turn the wrench to loosen and tighten the anchor bolt, and one hand to pull the cable through the anchor bolt. Since most people have only two hands, there is a special tool, called a third hand, to hold brake shoes against the rim. You don't really need one of these because a toe strap, piece of rope, or bungee cord wrapped around the caliper and tire will do the job as well.

The anchor bolt of a sidepull brake is usually keyed to the brake arm so it will not turn. This means you need only one wrench to turn the anchor bolt's nut. By contrast, the anchor bolt of a centerpull brake is on the yoke, which is held in place only by the cables. Use a pair of needle-nose pliers to simultaneously maintain the proper cable length and hold the yoke still while tightening.

The fine adjustment is made without tools, using a part called the *adjusting barrel*. The adjusting barrel is a bolt with a small hole drilled through it lengthwise and a larger hole drilled partway down. The inner wire goes all the way through the smaller hole, and the larger hole serves as a socket for the end of a length of cable housing.

On different bicycles, the adjusting barrels may be in different places but always at the end of a length of housing. With sidepull brakes, they are usually on the upper brake arms. Centerpull brakes generally locate them on the fulcrum at the top of the headset for the front brake and at the seatpost binder bolt for the rear brake. Sometimes they are on the brake levers, where the housing attaches to the hood.

The adjusting barrel operates by changing the effective length of the housing. It can be slightly confusing because turning it counterclockwise—the direction that normally loosens a bolt—makes the brake tighter. But don't worry about getting it backwards. Try turning it one way and then test the brake. If you find you have turned it the wrong way, just turn it the other way.

The adjusting barrel often has a locknut that you must loosen before the barrel will turn. Also, the barrel will be easier to turn if you squeeze the brake shoes against the rim with one hand to relieve the spring tension on the cable while you adjust

Photograph 4–7. Hold the cable and yoke still with a pair of needle-nose pliers while tightening the anchor bolt on centerpull brakes.

the barrel with the other hand. If you can't loosen the locknut by hand, use pliers.

When you have run out of range on the fine adjustment, it is time to change the coarse adjustment. As the cable stretches and brake shoes wear, the adjusting barrel will finally reach the point where you cannot turn it any farther without unscrewing it from the threaded piece that holds it. Before making the coarse adjustment, screw the adjusting barrel back in most of the way so you will be able to use the fine adjustment again afterwards. To allow for your coarse adjustment possibly being a little too tight, don't screw the adjusting barrel in quite all the way.

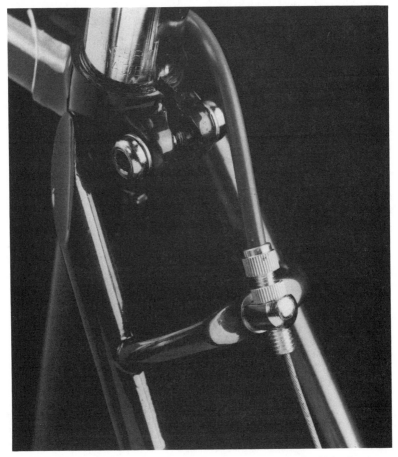

Photograph 4–8. The adjusting barrel on this centerpull brake is attached to a brazed-on brake cable bracket.

Brake Reach and Performance

Beyond cable adjustments and the choice of sidepull or centerpull brakes, several important factors affect the performance of your brakes. These factors have to do with the way the calipers and levers are set up and adjusted. As we stated earlier, centerpull brakes generally have higher mechanical advantage than sidepulls. That is, a given amount of force on the lever is multiplied into a larger amount of force on the rim. This often makes centerpull brakes a better choice for tourists with baggage or wherever heavier braking is needed. But there are other factors that affect the force on the rim. Chief among these factors is brake reach. This is the distance from the brake mounting bolt at the fork crown or rear brake bridge down to the brake shoes at the rim.

Reach can be short—and often is—on a bicycle intended for use with skinny tires and no fenders, for example, a racing bicycle. Reach must be greater on a bicycle with fatter tires and fenders. Unfortunately, the longer the reach, the lower the mechanical advantage of the brake.

Centerpull brakes, with their inherently higher mechanical advantage, are generally preferable where reach is long. Their pivots are lower, shortening the shoe ends of the brake arms. If a brake is required to work at too long a reach, it will work weakly despite feeling stiff through the levers. It is also much more likely to squeal or buzz as the longer arms flex forward and back. Many folding bikes, utility one-speeds, and BMX bikes with fat tires suffer from these problems.

Centerpull brakes help counteract the problems of long reach, but in extreme cases, the best choice is cantilever brakes, whose mechanical advantage does not depend on reach. For this reason, they are used on many tandems, particularly fat-tired touring tandems. A cantilever brake works like a centerpull, except that it has shorter, stiffer brake arms whose pivots are brazed directly to the fork blades or rear stays of the bicycle. This pivot mounting increases stiffness, and because the brake arms do not arch over the tire, the mechanical advantage can be high even when cantilever brakes are used with fat tires and fenders.

High mechanical advantage has a price though; a multipli-

Photograph 4–9. The arms on a cantilever brake are shorter and stiffer than those on a regular centerpull brake. The arm pivots are brazed directly to the fork blades.

cation of force between lever and caliper is achieved only by a reduction in brake shoe travel. For example, if one pound of force on the brake lever puts four pounds of force on the rim, each brake shoe moves only one-quarter as far as the lever does. Clearly, then, if there is excessive flex or wasted motion anywhere in the brake system, the lever is likely to bottom out on the handlebar before the shoes grip very tightly.

Excessive flex may be caused by soft, compressible brake shoes, a stretched cable, a flimsy headset cable stop, a damaged cable housing, or springy brake arms. You can see it if you squeeze the brake lever slowly. Wasted motion is most commonly caused by the brake shoes' being adjusted too far away from the rim, either due to neglect or because the rim is out of true, making a loose adjustment necessary. Careful brake adjustment, truing of wheels, switching to less compressible brake shoes, and choosing stiffer brake arms are important ways to add stiffness to your system, thus making high mechanical advantages effective.

Apart from the other factors mentioned, all brakes work better with shorter reach, and it is always easy to find some brake that will work well with short reach. Inexpensive short-reach sidepulls such as Weinmann 500s work impressively well, far better than models that are identical except for their longer reach.

On any given frame or fork, reach can be changed most easily by using rims of a different size. Twenty-seven-inch wheels on a frame made for 700C wheels, or 700C wheels on a frame made for 26-inch wheels, can allow a very noticeable improvement in brake performance, particularly when clearances were large with the original wheels. The top tube and bottom bracket will be raised somewhat, and front wheel trail will be slightly increased, but it is usually possible to keep the same brakes when going from 26 × 1⅜-inch to 700C. Check to make sure the tire (and, if one is used, the fender) will clear the frame.

Other ways to alter reach are to install the drop bolt made by Campagnolo (for its rear brake only) or to make alterations in your bicycle frame. For example, a brake bridge could be brazed in a lower position on the seatstays, and a front fork with a different crown design could place the brake bolt hole lower without changing steering geometry.

Cable and Lever Adjustments

Changing the reach is not the only way to control the mechanical advantage of a brake. On a centerpull brake, a shorter transverse cable (the cable that connects the two brake arms) decreases the mechanical advantage but can often effect an improvement in performance if the brake feels too spongy at the lever. A longer transverse cable, on the other hand, can increase the power of the brake as long as the lever doesn't hit the handlebar. Longer transverse cables are usually sold for the rear brakes on mixte frames, but there is also room for them with most front centerpull brakes.

Moderate differences in mechanical advantage can also be found among different models of brake levers. If your brakes feel too spongy or if the present levers bottom out on the handlebars, try substituting levers with a lower mechanical advantage. If your brakes feel too stiff and are not powerful enough, switch to levers with a higher mechanical advantage. Remember, the mechanical advantage can be determined by noting the ratio between how far the lever moves in relation to the movement of the brake shoes. A lever that moves 1 inch to move the shoes ¼ inch has a higher mechanical advantage than a lever that only moves ⅞ inch to move the shoes ¼ inch.

Brake Quick-Releases

Some brake levers, notably Weinmann and Dia-Compe, have a quick-release fitting that allows the lever to open farther, spreading the brake shoes for easier wheel removal without requiring you to detach a brake shoe. This is a useful convenience, especially in conjunction with quick-release wheels.

Other brake quick-releases may be located at the headset or seatpost bolt cable stop with centerpull brakes, or on the caliper itself with sidepull brakes. With Mafac centerpulls, it is easy to unhook the transverse cable without tools. Weinmann and Dia-Compe lever quick-releases do not affect normal operation of the brakes (other than that you must reach farther for the levers). The other quick-releases either leave the brakes adjusted loosely or disable them completely if you forget to reset them; they are thus a bit dangerous in the hands of a forgetful user.

Brake Lever Position

Decide which hand is to operate the front brake. Unless you have already developed your habits, this should be the hand with the slower reaction, since too rapid and too firm an application of your front brake can flip you forward over your handlebars. This is particularly likely if your front brake is adjusted tighter than your rear brake. While it is true that locking a rear wheel will send you into a skid, this is easier for the novice rider to control than a sudden flip.

Safe braking actually calls for different brake applications in different situations; it is an acquired skill, difficult to describe verbally. Accomplished racers use their front brakes more than their rear brakes because of the quick reaction and control provided that way. However, racers generally apply brakes with a feather touch rather than a hard squeeze. Experienced riders only use their brakes occasionally, and they know how to shift their body weight back on the bike in emergency stops.

Until you master these techniques and develop a sensitive feel for both your brakes, the safest approach for you to take is to match your dominant hand with your rear brake. If your bike is not already set up this way, you can simply rearrange the match-up of cables and levers. Many brake levers have a slotted attachment for the brake cable that allows removal and switching of the cables without tools if you squeeze the brake shoes together with one hand.

The position of brake levers on the handlebars is also adjustable. A bolt inside the brake hood tightens the clamp that fastens each lever to the handlebars. You can see this bolt if you squeeze the lever, but usually you must remove the cable to get at it. Make sure this bolt is tight. Levers for dropped handlebars should have the hoods angled upward so you can rest your hands on their tops. You can brake lightly from this comfortable riding position.

So-called "safety" brake levers (more accurately called "extension levers"), which also allow you to brake from the tops of the handlebars, offer little added advantage and are, in fact, hazardous. Extension levers look sensible to a beginner who is afraid of not being able to reach the normal brake levers. Unfortunately, extension levers place the hands at the center of the handlebars, reducing steering control when it is most needed, in braking. The hand position on these levers is awkward.

The riding posture used with extension levers is inappropriate for hard braking; your weight is high up, and your arms are below you, threatening to send you flying over the handlebars. By contrast, when using normal levers, your arms are ahead of you, where they can support your body against its deceleration in braking. And many extension levers depress the normal brake levers partway, reducing the amount of braking power that is possible before the levers hit the handlebars. They may also interfere with your grasp of the main levers and make riding with your hands on the brake hoods difficult.

It is easy to remove most brands of extension levers by unscrewing the bolts that attach them. A stub will protrude from the inner end of each brake lever pivot bolt. Remove it with a hacksaw and install rubber brake hoods, which add a classy appearance to your bike and make the top braking position on the normal brake levers much more comfortable.

If you have arthritis or another neck problem that prevents tilting your head back, you may have trouble reaching the brake levers on your dropped handlebars. Also, if you ride less than about once per week, the muscles that hold your head up will not strengthen, and dropped handlebars will give you a sore neck every time you ride. In these cases, you might need to switch to flat handlebars. However, most people are better off with dropped handlebars and normal brake levers. They're more efficient and comfortable, once you're used to them. If you cannot comfortably reach the normal levers, the solution may simply be a shorter handlebar stem.

Most manufacturers make their 27-inch wheel bikes of all frame sizes with the same top tube length, so short people often get caught with brake levers that are too far away. The problem is especially severe for short women riding mixte frames. It is possible for a shorter person to straddle a mixte frame and to ride it with a lowered saddle position, but the handlebars will be much too far forward and too high. The rider may become totally dependent on extension levers.

If a shorter stem does not bring the handlebars close enough, two solutions are possible. One is to turn a short stem completely around so that it is backwards, bringing the handlebars even closer and lower. This can correct the riding position and make the brake levers reachable, though the bicycle will not maneuver as well; this is a stopgap solution. The best solution for the shorter person is a frame that really fits, generally one with 24-inch wheels rather than the usual 27-inch wheels.

Many short people also have trouble reaching their hands around standard-size brake levers. If you have this problem, order smaller "junior" levers at a bike shop. These levers are available from Weinmann, Mafac, and CLB, among other manufacturers.

Adjusting Brake Calipers and Replacing Brake Shoes

Several adjustments and equipment choices are essential to first-rate brake performance. Become familiar with them so you can tailor your brakes to your needs and keep them working safely and reliably. We'll begin with adjustments to the calipers.

The bearing pivots of the calipers, like all bearings, should be just loose enough to move freely. If they are too tight, the calipers will not open when the levers are released; if too loose, the brakes will be harder to control precisely and more likely to squeal, buzz, or grab. A brake's arms should not rock noticeably on their pivots if you depress the lever and try to wheel the bike forward and backward.

All sidepull brakes have adjustable pivots. Most have a double nut at the front. Oil the pivot and the nuts before adjusting. Using a narrow wrench on the rear nut and another wrench on the front nut, tighten them against each other to allow the arms just the right clearance so that they can operate without either excessive friction or slop. Some sidepulls, mostly on 3-speed bikes, have a screwdriver slot at the front. After loosening the nut at the rear of the brake bolt, use a screwdriver to make adjustments, then retighten the nut.

A few centerpull brakes have adjustable pivots. Usually these are adjusted by turning the pivot bolts. On most centerpull brakes, the pivot bolts should simply be tightened down hard— bearing clearance is preset—but be sure to oil the pivots occasionally.

If brakes are not properly centered over a tire rim, one shoe will drag on the rim as you ride, making the bike hard to pedal. Before centering the brake, make sure the rim is centered in the forks. The easiest way to check this is by slipping the index finger of each hand between the tire and the fork (or chainstay) on each side. Both fingers should go in equally far. If they do not, the wheel may have been sloppily installed. It may also be incorrectly dished, or the hub axle or frame may be bent. Any of these conditions will make your bike steer to one side and should be corrected.

Once the wheel is properly set, you can turn to the brake. If it is a centerpull brake, loosen the mounting nut, move the calipers to the correct position, then retighten the nut. When working on a sidepull brake, first tighten the cap nut and adjacent locknut against each other. Then, leaving one wrench in place, move the other to the rear mounting nut and turn both together to rotate the entire brake on its mounting bolt. Unfortunately, some brakes do not adjust; you must center them by bending one of the brake shoe return springs.

Always make sure the nut that holds the brake bolt to the frame is tight. If it comes loose and the brake dangles by its cable into the wheel, you could go over the handlebars. There should be a washer under the nut, unless it is a modern self-locking nut with a nylon insert that grips the bolt.

Photograph 4–10. Adjust the brake so that the arms are just free enough to pivot, then tighten the two locking nuts against each other.

Photograph 4–11. With a wrench at each end, rotate the entire brake on its pivot bolt until it is centered.

Once the brake arms are properly positioned, you can turn your attention to the pads and shoes. The brake pads are the rubber-like blocks attached to the calipers, which rub against the rims to stop the bicycle. The brake shoes are the stamped-metal holders for the brake pads. The position of the pads is adjusted by means of the nuts that hold them to the brake arms. The pads should be adjusted so that they have the largest possible area of contact with the metal rim. They must not touch the tire or they will wear it out in no time at all.

Most brake pads have some sort of tread pattern facing the rim. If the pads are worn down past this pattern, or if there is less than about ⅛ inch of the pads protruding above their metal holder, they should be replaced. Actually, if your brake pads are more than three or four years old, you should probably replace them even if they are not worn out. Recent improvements in the rubber-like materials used in pads make newer ones more effective than the older ones, especially under wet conditions.

There are two methods for fastening brake shoes to brake arms. Most manufacturers equip their shoes with a threaded post. This post fits into a slot on the brake arm and is secured with a nut, but Mafac and a few other brands use an unthreaded post that fits into a hole in a special bolt on the brake arm. So be sure you get the right type of shoes for your brakes.

The Mafac-type mounting allows the shoe to be tilted up and down to match the angle of the rim sidewall. The easiest way to make this adjustment is to squeeze the brake lever with one hand. This will clamp the brake shoe against the rim while you tighten the holding nut on the caliper with your other hand. Make sure that the unthreaded post is as far into the mounting bolt as it will go. Otherwise it might slip when you apply the brake hard.

Brake shoes with threaded posts (except Mathauser shoes with special curved washers) cannot be adjusted to the rim angle, and even Mafac shoes cannot be adjusted for toe-in—that is, making the front end of the shoe contact the rim slightly before the rear end. Toe-in is important because it helps keep the brakes from squealing and grabbing the rim. If brakes are toed out so the rear edge of the brake pad contacts the rim first, the force from the rim flexes the caliper and briefly increases the toe-out. The pad then jumps back to its original position and degree of toe-out. The quick repetition of this cycle produces a squealing noise.

A common way to adjust toe-in is to bend the brake calipers with pliers or other metal-eating tools. Good mechanics routinely do this when assembling new bikes because brakes often have as much as two millimeters of toe-out. But for minor or repeated adjustments of toe-in/out, don't keep bending your brake calipers. Repeated bending can reduce a caliper's life, with the possibility of its cracking at a later date.

A better way to eliminate toe-out, one that also adjusts the tilt of the brake pad's face for maximum contact with the rim, is as follows. Run a piece of sandpaper in between the brake shoe and the rim—sandy side out—while squeezing the lever lightly. Sand the pad in this manner to conform to contours of the rim. This procedure will not produce toe-in, but normal wear and tear causes toe-in to disappear anyway. This procedure will make your brakes much less likely to squeal.

Some older brake shoes have removable rubber pads that can slide out of their dovetail holders. The holders have one open end and one closed end. It is essential that this type of brake shoe be installed so the closed end is forward; otherwise, the force of your braking can cause the pads to slide out of the shoes.

Once you have installed the type of brake arms, pads, and levers that best meet your needs, you can concentrate your attention on routine maintenance. At least every six months, you should check on the condition of your brake blocks. Clean and adjust them if they are still good; replace them if they are hard or worn. At least once a year, remove your brake cables from their housings for inspection and lubrication, and before every ride, make sure your brakes are adjusted for safe and sure performance. Attention to these details will enable you to ride with confidence.

Glossary

adjustable cup—cup section of bearing mechanism that can be tightened or loosened to eliminate either binding or play in bearings

adjusting barrel—a hollow bolt through which brake cable passes; used to make final adjustments in the length of the cable housing

Allen wrench—hexagonal-tipped tool that fits inside object to be adjusted

anaerobic adhesive—an adhesive used on fitted metal parts to prevent them from loosening

anchor bolt—bolt used to hold the cable on the arm of a rim brake

angle-adjusting screw—screw located at the dropout tab for adjusting the angle at which a rear derailleur extends beneath the dropout

antiseize compound—lubricating substance that prevents threaded parts from sticking to one another

axle—main shaft around which parts revolve, as in wheel hubs and crankset

bearings—hardened steel balls that roll easily; found in head-set, bottom bracket, wheel hubs, pedals, and freewheel

bottom bracket—cylinder in which crank spindle rotates; term often used to refer to entire assembly of cranks, spindle, and bearings

brake cable bridge—a thin metal bracket brazed onto the seatstays above a brake to hold the cable housing

brake cable hanger—a metal bracket that hangs from the seat bolt or the headset to hold the cable housing on centerpull brakes

brake pad—rubber-like block that presses against the rim to slow or stop the wheel from moving

brake shoe—metal part that holds the brake pad

Brinell hardness test—technique devised by Swedish engineer to test hardness of metal by pressing metal ball into the specimen

brinelling—circular indentations on a crown race caused by pressure from ball bearings

caged balls—ball bearings held in a ring or retainer that allows them to be installed and removed as a single unit

caliper brakes—hand-operated rim brakes with a pivotal arm on each side of the tire

cantilever brakes—rim brakes with pivoting arms mounted on fittings attached to seatstays or fork blades

centerpull brakes—rim brakes in which main cable connects with transverse cable, which pulls up on both arms simultaneously

chain cage—derailleur part through which chain passes

chain cage pivot—pin in a rear derailleur on which the two pulleys and the cage that houses them pivot back and forth as chain length is altered

chainring—see chainwheel

chain rivet extractor—a threaded pin tool for pressing out the rivets to remove a chain

chainstays—the two tubes that run horizontally from the bottom bracket to the rear dropouts

chainwheel (chainring)—sprocket attached to right crankarm to drive the chain

chainwheel fixing bolt—fasteners that hold chainweel to crankarm

clincher—a tire whose edges hook under the curved-in edge of a rim

coaster brake—foot-operated hub brake activated by back pedaling

cog—rear sprocket attached to the freewheel

cone—part of bearing race that fits inside the circle of balls (opposite a cup)

cone wrench—special thin wrench for adjusting cones on wheel hubs

cottered crank—crankset in which the crankarms are mounted on the circular ends of the bottom bracket spindle and held in place by cotter pins

cotterless crank—crankset in which the crankarms are forced onto tapered square or splined ends of the bottom bracket spindle and fastened to the spindle ends with recessed bolts

cotter pin—small wedge pin used to hold crankarm on bottom bracket spindle

cotter press—tool used to install or remove cotter pins from crankarm

crankarm—rotating arm that transfers pressure from pedal to chainwheel

crankarm bolt spanner—wrench used for removing crankarm fixing bolt on cotterless crankset

crankarm puller—special pressing tool used to remove crankarms from the spindle on cotterless cranks

crankset—bottom bracket spindle, bearings, crankarms, and chainwheels

crank spindle—axle of the bottom bracket whose ends hold the crankarms

crown—see fork crown

crown race—cone or circular bearing race attached to the fork at the bottom of the fork stem

C-spanner—wrench with C-shaped end, used for tightening bottom bracket lockring

cup—part of bearing race that fits around the circle of balls (opposite a cone)

derailleur—mechanism that forces a moving chain from one sprocket to another for the purpose of changing gears

derailleur cage—see chain cage

dish—adjustment of spokes on rear wheel that offsets the hub to allow room for the freewheel while keeping the wheel centered between the dropouts

down tube—the tube running from the headset to the bottom bracket

dropout—slots into which rear wheel axle fits

dropout hanger—metal bracket extending below right dropout for attaching rear derailleur

dustcap—cap that screws into crankarm over the ends of the bottom bracket spindle to protect the threads used when removing crankarms

expander wedge—a mechanism that, when stem bolt is tightened, pulls up inside split tube creating pressure that holds stem in place

ferrule—a short tube, ring, or cap put on the end of a slender shaft to prevent it from splitting

fixed cup—the right-hand cup of a bottom bracket, screwed to a fixed position in the frame and left in place during bottom bracket overhauls

fork—tubed part of bicycle that holds a wheel

fork crown (crown)—horizontal piece on top of the fork that connects the blades to the fork stem

fork rake—the shortest distance between the front wheel axle and the line of the head tube extended downward

fork stem—see steerer tube, steering column

freewheel—the ratchet mechanism on the rear hub that allows the wheel to rotate faster than the chain

fulcrum—unmoving part that gives moving parts leverage

gear ratio—calculated by multiplying the diameter of the rear wheel in inches by the number of teeth on the chainwheel divided by the number of teeth on the rear cog

headset—the bearing mechanism in the head tube consisting of the races, cups, cones, balls, and locknuts

head tube—the tube of the frame in which the front fork is mounted

hub—the central part of a wheel, including the axle, bearings, and shell to hold the moving parts

hub brake—any brake mechanism that operates through the wheel hub

jockey pulley—disc over which the chain passes; the upper wheel in a rear derailleur

left-hand thread—tightens in a counterclockwise direction and loosens in a clockwise direction

locknut—a nut screwed down hard on another to prevent it from loosening

lug—metal sleeve on a frame that holds tubes together at joints

mechanical advantage—for rim brakes, the ratio between the force on the levers and the force on the brake shoes; the greater distance travelled by the lever in relation to the movement of the shoes, the less lever force needed to move the shoes, hence their greater mechanical advantage

mixte frame—frame with no top tube but instead two long tubes extending from the top of the head tube to the rear fork ends; commonly referred to as a ladies' frame

parallelogram mechanism—parallel metal plates on a rear derailleur that allow the pulleys to move horizontally along a single plane

pedal spindle—axle that supports the pedal and around which it spins

pin spanner—tool with two pins to fit into holes in bottom bracket adjustable cup, used to tighten and loosen the cup

Presta valve—valve commonly found on tubular tires; has no inner spring, but a threaded pin that must be loosened to allow inflation with special pump

quick-release brakes—brakes equipped with a device that allows the cable to be temporarily lengthened so the pads can be moved apart for quick removal or replacement of a wheel

quick-release hub (or axle)—hollow axle on wheel with skewer rod running through center, a nut attached to one end, and a hand-operated cam on the other; allows quick removal and replacement of wheel

race—circle inside cups and cones that bearing balls contact as they roll

right-hand thread—tightens in a clockwise direction and loosens in a counterclockwise direction

rim—metal circle on wheels that holds tire and is attached to the spokes

saddle—seat of the bicycle

Schrader valve—tire valve with inner spring that depresses to allow inflation; similar to valves found on auto tires

seatpost—pipe-shaped part, inserted into seat tube, to which saddle is attached

seat tube—tube into which the seatpost fits; runs from top tube down to bottom bracket

sew-up tire—tire with an inner tube stitched inside the casing; also called a tubular

sidepull brake—rim brake in which cable attaches to one side but both arms pivot on a single bolt

skewer—tension rod that extends through a quick-release hub

spokes—wires that hold the hub in the center of the rim to which they transfer the load

sprocket—wheel or cylinder with teeth to engage a chain

steering column (fork stem)—pipe that extends above the front fork, turns inside the head tube, and holds the handlebar stem

stem—tube that holds the handlebars and extends into the inside of the head tube and steering column

third hand—spring tool used to hold brake arms together during installation or adjustment of a cable

top tube—horizontal tube on bicycle frame that runs from top of head tube to top of seat tube

transverse cable (yoke cable)—short piece of cable whose ends are attached to the two arms and whose center connects with the main cable of a centerpull brake

true wheel—state in which the wheel's edge is perfectly circular, all in one plane, and the axle is at the center

tubular—type of pneumatic tire that has inner tube stitched inside

yoke—a small metal piece shaped like an upside-down Y that connects the main cable with the transverse cable on a centerpull brake

yoke cable—see transverse cable

Credits

The information in this book is drawn from these and other articles from *Bicycling* magazine.

"How to Take Care of Your Bike—All Year Long"   Tim Wilhelm, "How to Take Care of Your Bike—All Year Long," *Bicycling,* January/February 1981, pp. 95–97.

"Overhauling Hubs"   Tim Wilhelm, "Overhauling Hubs," *Bicycling,* May 1981, pp. 86–90.

"Miles Ahead: Headset Care and Maintenance"   Jeff Davis, "Miles Ahead: Headset Care and Maintenance," *Bicycling,* September/October 1983, pp. 108–19.

"Cottered Crank Removal"   Sheldon C. Brown, "Tool Tips: Cottered Crank Removal," *Bicycling,* January/February 1983, pp. 126–31.

"Overhaul Your Bottom Bracket"   Tim Wilhelm, "Overhaul Your Bottom Bracket—Do This Once a Year At Least," *Bicycling,* January/February 1981, pp. 89–94.

"For Better Shifting—Tune Up Your Rear Derailleur" John S. Allen and Sheldon C. Brown, "For Better Shifting—Tune Up Your Rear Derailleur," *Bicycling,* June 1983, pp. 150–60.

"Know Your Brakes"   Sheldon C. Brown and John S. Allen, "Know Your Brakes: Part One," *Bicycling,* December 1981, pp. 89–97; "Know Your Brakes: Part Two," *Bicycling,* January/February 1982, pp. 97–109.

Photos and Illustrations

Sheldon C. Brown: photos 3–1 and 4–3; Mark Lenny: photo 1–2; Photo Dept., Rodale Press: photo 3–2; Christie C. Tito: photos 2–4, 2–5, 2–6, 2–7, 4–2, and 4–9; Sally Shenk Ullman: photos 1–1, 1–3, 2–1, 2–2, 2–3, 3–3, 3–4, 4–1, 4–4, 4–5, 4–6, 4–7, 4–8, 4–10, and 4–11. George Retseck: illustration 3–1.